We Can Fix It!
Reclaiming the American Dream

V. O. Diedlaff

Copyright © 2018 V. O. Diedlaff
All rights reserved
diedlaffing.blogspot.com

1 Income Inequality, 2 Democracy, 3 Neuropsychology
ISBN: ISBN-13: 978-1987783056
ISBN-10: 1987783050

CONTENTS

On the Lifeboat	5
A Broken Dream	13
A Bit of History	19
A Middle Bulges Before Belts Tighten	43
The Robots Are Coming	59
The Silenced Majority	71
Follow the Money	81
Cooperation or Chaos	93
Know Your Enemy	99
Weapons of Mass Deception	109
Getting Even	127
Book and Journal Sources	137
Web Sources	141

On the Lifeboat

When a man wants to rob a bank he hides behind a mask, but when a banker wants to rob a man, he hides behind a corporation.

The United States is now in its second year of divisive and dysfunctional political turmoil. Even-tempered social discourse has been largely replaced by a circus—a frightening and dangerous one—but a circus just the same. People are entertained but not informed. They're fed news that's both popular and engaging, yet unsubstantial like junk food. Good information is out there, but it doesn't reach many because the circus distracts them. We cannot ignore the circus—it shows us threats that must be taken seriously. However, the circus keeps us overly-focused on sensational events, rather than on the serious, little noticed, underlying issues that urgently need our attention. Let me illustrate those issues in a parable.

A royal family once set out for an important destination in order to enhance their wealth, fame, and reputations. Before they could reach their destination, their ship sank. While many drowned, the royal family was safely put aboard a lifeboat along with two viziers and a rowing crew.

Spotting land to the north, the coxswain set his crew to rowing against the strong southerly current. The viziers set about ensuring the royal family's welfare.

We Can Fix It

When they finished, they conferred with the coxswain. After hearing his news, they determined that they'd run short of rations on their final day at sea.

The viziers reported the situation to the king. The king looked at the queen and the royal children and addressed the viziers with a scowl, "Do you mean to say that my darlings must be deprived of food for an entire day? Why can't they row faster?"

And, so the viziers returned to the coxswain and told him to get his crew rowing faster. The coxswain tried this for a day before informing the viziers that they'd gained a one meal advantage over royal hunger. The royal family would only miss two meals instead of three. The viziers conferred and told the coxswain to have the rowers work longer shifts.

Two more days passed, then the coxswain reported, "My crew is exhausted, but if we can keep up this pace the royal family will now only miss one meal."

The viziers brought this good news to the king, but he became angry rather than glad. "I refuse to allow the royal family to miss even a single meal." The viziers conferred and decided that since the coxswain only set the pace, and did no actual rowing, he wasn't essential. They threw him from the boat, certain that reduced middle management would solve their problem.

Without a coxswain, the viziers took turns calling out the rowing pace. But as sometimes happens when managers have ample theoretical knowledge but little of the hands-on kind, efficiency decreased and the lifeboat barely made progress against the strong southerly

On the Lifeboat

current. When the two viziers realized that the royal family would miss two meals instead of only one, they pitched a rower from the boat. The remaining rowers struggled to do the lost man's work as well as their own, but because of his absence they now needed to correct course more often. The viziers addressed the problem of broken symmetry by pitching the lost rower's former partner from the lifeboat as well. The next day the procedure was repeated and another two rowers were put off the boat.

I think you see where this is going. Ultimately, the lifeboat drifted south instead of keeping to its northerly course. Some weeks later, searchers found a lifeboat full of well-fed royal corpses far to the south. The royal family had all died of exposure to the harsh equatorial sun.

In this parable, the royal family is America's wealthy elite, the viziers are the politicians they've bought, and the rowing crew is the American people. The "harsh equatorial sun" of the parable is the climate change that will affect us all. Climate change may be the greatest threat to America and all of humanity. However, people underestimate this threat because climate change is considered a long-term threat. There are related and more-immediate threats putting average Americans at economic risk. The cause of all these threats is an unimaginative and undisciplined greed.

Perhaps you don't believe that climate change is real, perhaps you need more evidence. If that's the case, I recommend you watch the episode on Venus from the series "Cosmos." I believe you'll be convinced in less than an hour. If you're still not convinced, let me ask you a question. According to *Nasa.gov*, only three percent of articles appearing in peer-reviewed science journals reject the reality of climate change. If you were a gambler, would you stake your children's welfare on a long-shot bet that climate change might prove false? Regardless of how you answered this question, some of the same forces that slow efforts to limit climate change are also keeping your wages low, putting your home, wealth and health at risk, and endangering our society.

The forces that are crippling our country both cause and result from extreme income inequality. One result of extreme income inequality is the high level of poverty in America. According to Philip Alston, writing on *Ohchr.org*, for the United Nations in December 2017, more than one in eight Americans lives in poverty. Nearly half of these have incomes of less than half of the amount set as the poverty level.

Extreme income inequality brings both extreme poverty and extreme wealth. It also depresses the buying power and economic security of those with middling incomes. Roughly 90 percent of America's wealth is currently controlled by its wealthiest 20 percent. This is today's side of income inequality. Tomorrow's side will be worse, both because inequality is increasing and because the efforts of some of America's wealthiest have slowed and continue to slow efforts to address climate change. According to Paul Barrett and Matthew Philips writing on

On the Lifeboat

Bloomberg.com, ExxonMobil knew about climate change in 1977, but chose to deny it. More recently, the Trump administration implemented a tariff on solar panels that some experts, including Joshua Rhodes writing on *Forbes.com,* say will cause 23,000 jobs to be lost in 2018 and will cripple the U.S. solar industry in the longer term. Correctly implemented, a tariff could help the domestic solar industry, but this tariff will hurt it instead. Perhaps that's its intention. Suspiciously, the tariff expires at the same time as does the solar Investment Tax Credit.

During the Cold War, *competition* was often cited as the factor that gave Capitalism its edge over Communism. But Capitalism isn't always competitive, therefore monopolies are restrained or broken in order to restore companies' ability to compete. Competition also implies risk, something worth taking for possible gain, but worth avoiding when it could bring loss. ExxonMobil chose to avoid risk by concealing climate change rather than by taking risks that would have gained it a competitive advantage as an early investor in renewable energy.

For the already wealthy it makes sense to maintain and grow wealth by minimizing competition and risk. For these people, it makes sense to influence the political process and change laws to gain competitive advantages and reduce risks. Since the early 1980s, some of America's wealthiest people and corporations have increasingly done so through political action committees (PACs), lobbyists and think tanks.

We Can Fix It

While income inequality affects personal budgets and well-being, its darker side is the ability it gives the wealthy to shape the American political dialog. Consider the Tax Cuts and Jobs Act of 2017. It's been promoted as a tax cut for the middle class. But is it really? Although only one in four Americans think the tax act is a good idea, wealthy political donors like Charles Koch hope to convince you that you'll benefit from the tax act. Writing on *Washingtonpost.com* in January 2018, Michelle Ye Hee Lee reported that the Koch network plans to spend up to 40 million dollars promoting the tax act's benefits. Why would a donor network do this? Because its members stand to benefit the most. Those who earn over a million dollars will see tax cuts of 3.3 percent in 2018 while those earning between $50,000 and $75,000 will see cuts of only 1.6 percent, less than half as much. When the tax cuts expire, this same group will pay about $30 more in taxes, while those earning over one million dollars will continue to see reduced taxes, albeit a mere 0.9 percent instead of 2018's 3.3 percent, according to a post by Danielle Kurtzleben on *Npr.org*. Elected officials ignored the will of the majority and instead followed the will of wealthy donors. A class warfare tax act is the result.

Blend together a co-opted cohort of politicians, a wealthy elite clinging to an anachronistic and soulless doctrine, extreme income inequality, and deteriorating employment prospects for the majority—and you have a recipe for social disaster. But the coming disaster won't

On the Lifeboat

be merely social—it will be environmental as well. What we fail to fix today will impact our decedents for hundreds of years to come. So let's get to work reclaiming our democracy from those who would steal it from us.

A Broken Dream

But what improves the circumstances of the greater part, can never be regarded as any inconveniency to the whole. No society can surely be flourishing and happy, of which the far greater part of the members are poor and miserable. —Adam Smith

Are you one of millions of Americans whose struggles to live the American Dream have paid off in financial nightmares? It's not the fault of the dream and it's not your fault either. It's a good dream and it worked once upon a time. But today it's broken. This book is about how the dream broke, who broke it, and how you can fix it. The dream must be fixed, and fixed soon, because if we don't fix it, our people will experience massive suffering and possible social collapse.

Just what is the American Dream? It's the idea that anyone, if they're diligent, clever and work hard can achieve success—upward mobility is achievable for those who are tenacious, thrifty and bold. The dynamics of the Dream will be discussed in a later chapter. For now let me state my main theme: Income Inequality is the greatest current threat to the American Dream. When some contemporary writers use the term income inequality, their intended meaning is *extreme income and wealth inequality* and that was my intention in the sentence above. Some argue that income inequality occurs naturally and is of no great concern. They are partially correct. Inequality must exist in a competitive economic system in order to motivate competition. Yet such systems can become unbalanced. During many eras, income inequality wasn't a major social problem. At other times, income inequality impacted social welfare. Ours is such a time. Income equality has been growing in severity since the 1980s and today it's a dangerous social threat. Statistics presented by *Oecd.org* show that the United States has higher income inequality than most other advanced nations.

    The founders of our country were perfectly aware that income inequality existed. They accepted it as a natural element of human society. They never intended to create a society in which every citizen had an equal share of income and ownership, but they did desire a level field on which citizens would play out their lives. On such a field every player has the same opportunities. On an unlevel field, advantaged players can move easily while disadvantaged players must struggle uphill. The American Dream just isn't possible unless there is a largely level playing field. Let's examine what two of our presidents said about the American Dream.

    These excerpts come from a letter that Thomas Jefferson, serving in France, wrote to James Madison. His initial comments refer to the extreme inequality in France, but they could just as easily apply to current conditions in the United States. Since farming was a major occupation during Jefferson's time, he speaks primarily about property. Today most Americans don't

A Broken Dream

grow their own food, but money can easily be substituted for property in this quote. In his letter, Jefferson anticipates inheritance tax, graduated income tax, and social welfare policies:

> I am conscious that an equal division of property is impracticable, but the consequences of this enormous inequality producing so much misery to the bulk of mankind. ... The descent of property of every kind therefore to all the children, or to all the brothers and sisters, or other relations in equal degree, is a politic measure and a practicable one. Another means of silently lessening the inequality of property is to exempt all from taxation below a certain point, and to tax the higher portions or property in geometrical progression as they rise. Whenever there are in any country uncultivated lands and unemployed poor, it is clear that the laws of property have been so far extended as to violate natural right. The earth is given as a common stock for man to labor and live on. If for the encouragement of industry we allow it to be appropriated, we must take care that other employment be provided to those excluded from the appropriation. If we do not, the fundamental right to labor the earth returns to the unemployed. It is too soon yet in our country to say that every man who cannot find employment, but who can find uncultivated land, shall be at liberty to cultivate it, paying a moderate rent. But it is not too soon to provide by every possible means that as few as possible shall be without a little portion of land. The small landholders are the most precious part of a state.

We Can Fix It

Land was still plentiful when Abraham Lincoln spoke these words 74 years later, two years before the Civil War began:

> The prudent, penniless beginner in the world, labors for wages awhile, saves a surplus with which to buy tools or land, for himself; then labors on his own account another while, and at length hires another new beginner to help him. This, say its advocates, is free labor—the just and generous, and prosperous system, which opens the way for all—gives hope to all, and energy, and progress, and improvement of condition to all. If any continue through life in the condition of the hired laborer, it is not the fault of the system, but because of either a dependent nature which prefers it, or improvidence, folly, or singular misfortune.

When Lincoln said these words to the Wisconsin State Agricultural Society in 1859, small farms were more common than large corporate organizations. Although such organizations played a smaller part in the overall economy, Lincoln spoke the words above in opposition to what he named the "mud-sill" theory. That theory goes like this:

> By some it is assumed that labor is available only in connection with capital—that nobody labors, unless somebody else owning capital, somehow, by the use of it, induces him to do it. Having assumed this, they proceed to consider whether it is best that capital shall hire laborers, and thus induce them to work by their own consent, or buy them, and drive them to it, without their consent. Having proceeded so far, they naturally conclude that all

A Broken Dream

laborers are necessarily either hired laborers, or slaves. They further assume that whoever is once a hired laborer, is fatally fixed in that condition for life; and thence again, that his condition is as bad as, or worse, than that of a slave. This is the 'mud-sill' theory. But another class of reasoners hold the opinion that there is no such relation between capital and labor, as assumed; and that there is no such thing as a freeman being fatally fixed for life, on the condition of a hired laborer, that both these assumptions are false, and all inferences from them groundless. They hold that labor is prior to, and independent of, capital; that, in fact, capital is the fruit of labor, and could never have existed if labor had not first existed—that labor can exist without capital, but that capital could never have existed without labor. Hence they hold that labor is the superior—greatly the superior of capital.

    Clearly Lincoln believed in the American Dream, yet he was aware that there were those who posed a threat to that dream. That threat didn't fully emerge until the industrial revolution took firm hold in the United States shortly after Lincoln's death.

    Our American Dream matters. It defines our ambitions and possibilities. But dreams are only useful when they can guide our waking lives. When this happens we're able to lead productive and satisfying lives. However when conditions change and dreams can no longer be achieved, we must either abandon those dreams or change those conditions. Change is the better choice and we can accomplish this. To do so we must first understand the conditions under which the Dream works and those conditions under which it breaks.

Our media, television, newsprint, radio, and the web readily supply us with information. Far more information than was available to us over past centuries. Like the confusion of tongues that occurred at Babel in Genesis 11, we face a confusion of information and it's dividing our country. With so much information surrounding us, opportunists find new ways to get their messages out. They've learned that we don't have the time to read, discuss, and think deeply as our nation's founders did. So they shorten their narratives and find ways of grabbing our attention. To be heard, to change what we believe, they go straight for our guts instead of our brains. With the right packaging they can insert lies into the Dream, sabotaging it from within. And that's just what they're doing. To better understand who those opportunists are and how they're destroying the Dream, the next chapter will review a bit of history.

A Bit of History

The most effective way to destroy people is to deny and obliterate their own understanding of their history. —George Orwell

The most serious threat to America's constitutional government is the narrowing of its middle class, claims Ganesh Sitaraman in his 2017 book, *The crisis of the middle class constitution: why economic inequality threatens our Republic.* He argues that, "From the ancient Greeks onward, political philosophers were preoccupied with the problem of economic inequality and its relationship to the structure of government. The wealthy elites would clash with everyone else—the rich oppressing the poor, the poor seeking to confiscate and redistribute the wealth of the rich. Economic inequality led inevitably to political inequality and, as a result, instability, class warfare, and constitutional revolution."

Sitaraman continues: "The great republics throughout history—Rome, Florence, Venice, England—all had what we think of as *class warfare constitutions,* governments designed on the assumption that economic inequality was inevitable and the clash between rich and poor inescapable." For this reason, "Class warfare constitutions took as a premise that inequality would exist in society, and because inequality was a threat to stable government, they built checks into the constitutional structure itself."

We Can Fix It

The founders of the United States chose not to write a class warfare constitution. Because land was plentiful, and because incomes were relatively equal, the framers wrote a "*middle-class constitution.*" For this reason, claims Sitaraman, "[O]ur Constitution assumes relative economic equality in society; it assumes that the middle class is and will remain dominant." This worked well early in our country's history when land was plentiful and before industrialization roared across the nation—like the steam engine—carrying some in opulence but leaving others in poverty. Sitaraman notes:

> During the time of the American Revolution, through the era of the Articles of Confederation, and into the ratification period and the Early Republic, there was a robust and strong belief that a truly republican form of government was only possible in a society with relative economic equality. Drawing on a long tradition in political philosophy, the founding generation understood that the balance of political power had to mirror the balance of economic power in society. As a result, there were only two stable ways to design a government: Where there was inequality, there had to be a class warfare constitution. When there was relative equality in society, there could be a commonwealth or Republic. Unlike Europe, with its hereditary nobility, property rules that concentrated wealth, and history of feudalism, America didn't have centuries of entrenched wealth or poverty. With vast lands to the west and the possibility of education, any white man (at the time, of course, it was limited as such)

A Bit of History

had the opportunity to access the middle class.

A great deal of discussion occurred before our constitution was written. Ultimately, our founders decided not to pen a class warfare constitution with a House of Commons and a House of Lords. They had no desire to preserve an aristocracy. Instead they penned a middle-class constitution with two classless houses forming a Congress. But doubts remained. During the 1790s, Jefferson and Madison argued over issues regarding the creation of a national bank. Similar issues continued this debate during Jackson's presidency. Luckily, the United States had ample land, which functioned like a "safety valve," releasing a build-up of excess steam generated by income inequality. For a time, the valve worked, "... Americans in the early republic remained relatively equal economically, and they understood their equality as a function of their geography. With land readily available to the west, Americans believed they had a 'safety valve,' even as wage labor started to displace land as a source of productivity."

By the late nineteenth century, land once thought unlimited had become scarce. Rural populations had migrated to cities and become wage laborers in an industrializing nation. Much of the nation's wealth had shifted into corporate hands. This was the Gilded Age, a period that ran from about 1870 to the turn of the century. It was a time of great wealth—for some—the Robber Barons. The name was no coincidence. They were called robbers because many were notorious for corruptly gaming capitalism to benefit themselves. For those who were laborers rather than industrialists, life could be difficult.

To some degree, the writer Horatio Alger Jr. can be thanked for popularizing the American Dream. His successful fourth book, *Ragged Dick*, became the pattern for the numerous others which followed. His books for boys were rags-to-riches fictions in which poverty is overcome when a youth's good character and hard work draw attention from a successful mentor who offers the opportunity for him to make something of himself. *Ragged Dick* was published in 1868 just as the Gilded Age was getting underway. But for many during this period, becoming a self-made man became more difficult as did the hope of upward mobility. Let me quote from Steve Fraser's *The Age of Acquiescence : The Life and Death of American Resistance to Organized Wealth and Power*:

> Downward mobility ... is the underground, invisible story of industrial Progress, the counterpoint to the widely celebrated tale of upward mobility at the heart of the American mythos. And it left its mark not only on the 'lower orders'—struggling farmers, peasant immigrants, dispossessed, déclassé handicraftsmen—but also among middling merchants, storekeepers, and petty producers in towns and small cities across the nation. They succumbed to the relentless pressures of the giant corporation. Often enough, that corporation was erected on their remains, sometimes absorbing their facilities, their personnel, or else leaving all that bankrupt and inert by the side of the road. Or just as frequently those small businessmen devoured one another or effectively committed suicide, driven to compete close to and then past the point of economic survival. Their death cleared the market, opened up the way for enormous industrial combines, raw materials producers, mass market distributors, nationwide transportation and communications corporations, the champions of

A Bit of History

consolidated capital accumulation and the integrated national marketplace—all the purveyors of Progress.

In the early days of America, economic self-sufficiency was easily achieved. Steve Fraser reports that 80 percent of Americans were self-employed in 1820. But by 1940, only 20 percent of the population was self-employed. What happened? Industrialization was responsible for a loss of worker self-sufficiency and its replacement with dependency on large employers. It's said that a rising tide lifts all ships. That's true. The industrial revolution improved living standards for society overall, but it economically dislocated citizens individually. Hoards of individuals, like small boats, were unable to navigate the newly dangerous waters and, as a result, sank into poverty.

Fraser claims many suffered, noting that, "Some economic historians have described the whole last third of the century as one long depression, worldwide in scope, characterized by price deflation, mass bankruptcies, and declining rates of profit, interrupted by spasms of meteoric growth." Fraser lists five major depressions, the first in 1837 and the last in 1893. A sixth occurred in the next century in 1907.

During the late 1800s workers who desired a voice in determining their wages and working hours began to form and join labor unions. Their efforts had little effect before the century ended. Sitaraman says, "Economic power grew increasingly concentrated in the hands of the few, and political power followed. Activists, thinkers, workers, and farmers tried to adapt the agrarian Republic of the founding to the industrial age, only to fall victim to Gilded Age plutocrats."

However, labor won more victories during the first half of the twentieth century. Early in that century,

We Can Fix It

Theodore Roosevelt spoke for the common man in his New Nationalism Speech. Roosevelt begins:

> We come here today to commemorate one of the epoch-making events of the long struggle for the rights of man—the long struggle for the uplift of humanity. Our country—this great republic—means nothing unless it means the triumph of a real democracy, the triumph of popular government, and, in the long run, of an economic system under which each man shall be guaranteed the opportunity to show the best that there is in him.

After his introduction, Roosevelt discusses two great crises in American history. The first resulted in the country's formation. The second led to the Civil War. He then offers some of Lincoln's words (previously quoted). Then he adds, "If that remark was original with me, I should be even more strongly denounced as a Communist agitator than I shall be anyhow. It is Lincoln's. I am only quoting it; and that is one side; that is the side the capitalist should hear. Now, let the working man hear his side."

But before I share those words, it's important to note that: 1) Although the industrial revolution didn't get well underway in the United States until after the Civil War, it began roughly three decades earlier in England. 2) Marx and Engels published their *Communist Manifesto* in England in 1848, several decades into England's industrial revolution. 3) However, the Bolsheviks didn't assume power in Russia until 1917 as World War I was winding down, seven years after Theodore Roosevelt's speech. While communists were condemned during Roosevelt's time, they were condemned far more vigorously during the Cold War following World War II. Roosevelt continues with final quotes from Lincoln:

A Bit of History

"Capital has its rights, which are as worthy of protection as any other rights. ... Nor should this lead to a war upon the owners of property. Property is the fruit of labor; ... property is desirable; is a positive good in the world."

And then comes a thoroughly Lincolnlike sentence:

"Let not him who is houseless pull down the house of another, but let him work diligently and build one for himself, thus by example assuring that his own shall be safe from violence when built."

It seems to me that, in these words, Lincoln took substantially the attitude that we ought to take; he showed the proper sense of proportion in his relative estimates of capital and labor, of human rights and property rights. Above all, in this speech, as in many others, he taught a lesson in wise kindliness and charity; an indispensable lesson to us of today. But this wise kindliness and charity never weakened his arm or numbed his heart. We cannot afford weakly to blind ourselves to the actual conflict which faces us today. The issue is joined, and we must fight or fail.

In every wise struggle for human betterment one of the main objects, and often the only object, has been to achieve in large measure equality of opportunity. ...

These additional excerpts from Roosevelt's speech show his fervency for preserving opportunities for all citizens regardless of their wealth, and with disregard for assumed privileges:

> At many stages in the advance of humanity, this conflict between the men who possess more than they have earned and the men who have earned more than they possess is the central condition of progress. In our day it appears as the struggle of freemen to gain and hold the right of self-government as against the special interests, who twist the methods of free government into machinery for defeating the popular will. At every stage, and under all circumstances, the essence of the struggle is to equalize opportunity, destroy privilege, and give to the life and citizenship of every individual the highest possible value both to himself and to the commonwealth. ...
>
> Practical equality of opportunity for all citizens, when we achieve it, will have two great results. First, every man will have a fair chance to make of himself all that in him lies; to reach the highest point to which his capacities, unassisted by special privilege of his own and unhampered by the special privilege of others, can carry him, and to get for himself and his family substantially what he has earned. Second, equality of opportunity means that the commonwealth will get from every citizen the highest service of which he is capable. No man who carries the burden of the special privileges of another can give to the commonwealth that service to which it is fairly entitled.
>
> I stand for the square deal. But when I say that

A Bit of History

I am for the square deal, I mean not merely that I stand for fair play under the present rules of the game, but that I stand for having those rules changed so as to work for a more substantial equality of opportunity and of reward for equally good service. ...

Now, this means that our government, national and state, must be freed from the sinister influence or control of special interests. Exactly as the special interests of cotton and slavery threatened our political integrity before the Civil War, so now the great special business interests too often control and corrupt the men and methods of government for their own profit. We must drive the special interests out of politics. That is one of our tasks today. Every special interest is entitled to justice—full, fair, and complete—and, now, mind you, if there were any attempt by mob-violence to plunder and work harm to the special interest, whatever it may be, that I most dislike, and the wealthy man, whomsoever he may be, for whom I have the greatest contempt, I would fight for him, and you would if you were worth your salt. He should have justice. For every special interest is entitled to justice, but not one is entitled to a vote in Congress, to a voice on the bench, or to representation in any public office. The Constitution guarantees protection to property, and we must make that promise good. But it does not give the right of suffrage to any corporation.

The true friend of property, the true conservative, is he who insists that property shall be the ser-

We Can Fix It

vant and not the master of the commonwealth; who insists that the creature of man's making shall be the servant and not the master of the man who made it. ...

There can be no effective control of corporations while their political activity remains. To put an end to it will be neither a short nor an easy task, but it can be done. ...

The absence of effective State, and, especially, national, restraint upon unfair money-getting has tended to create a small class of enormously wealthy and economically powerful men, whose chief object is to hold and increase their power. The prime need to is to change the conditions which enable these men to accumulate power which it is not for the general welfare that they should hold or exercise. We grudge no man a fortune which represents his own power and sagacity, when exercised with entire regard to the welfare of his fellows. ... So it is with us. We grudge no man a fortune in civil life if it is honorably obtained and well used. It is not even enough that it should have been gained without doing damage to the community. We should permit it to be gained only so long as the gaining represents benefit to the community. This, I know, implies a policy of a far more active governmental interference with social and economic conditions in this country than we have yet had, but I think we have got to face the fact that such an increase in governmental control is now necessary. ...

A Bit of History

No man should receive a dollar unless that dollar has been fairly earned. Every dollar received should represent a dollar's worth of service rendered—not gambling in stocks, but service rendered. The really big fortune, the swollen fortune, by the mere fact of its size acquires qualities which differentiate it in kind as well as in degree from what is possessed by men of relatively small means. Therefore, I believe in a graduated income tax on big fortunes, and in another tax which is far more easily collected and far more effective—a graduated inheritance tax on big fortunes, properly safeguarded against evasion, and increasing rapidly in amount with the size of the estate. ...

Nothing is more true than that excess of every kind is followed by reaction; a fact which should be pondered by reformer and reactionary alike. We are face to face with new conceptions of the relations of property to human welfare, chiefly because certain advocates of the rights of property as against the rights of men have been pushing their claims too far. The man who wrongly holds that every human right is secondary to his profit must now give way to the advocate of human welfare, who rightly maintains that every man holds his property subject to the general right of the community to regulate its use to whatever degree the public welfare may require it.

But I think we may go still further. The right to regulate the use of wealth in the public interest is universally admitted. Let us admit also the right to regulate the terms and conditions of labor, which is

We Can Fix It

the chief element of wealth, directly in the interest of the common good. The fundamental thing to do for every man is to give him a chance to reach a place in which he will make the greatest possible contribution to the public welfare. Understand what I say there. Give him a chance, not push him up if he will not be pushed. ... No man can be a good citizen unless he has a wage more than sufficient to cover the bare cost of living, and hours of labor short enough so after his day's work is done he will have time and energy to bear his share in the management of the community, to help in carrying the general load. We keep countless men from being good citizens by the conditions of life by which we surround them. We need comprehensive workman's compensation acts, both State and national laws to regulate child labor and work for women, and, especially, we need in our common schools not merely education in book-learning, but also practical training for daily life and work. ... Those who oppose reform will do well to remember that ruin in its worst form is inevitable if our national life brings us nothing better than swollen fortunes for the few and the triumph in both politics and business of a sordid and selfish materialism. ...

It is particularly important that all moneys received or expended for campaign purposes should be publicly accounted for, not only after election, but before election as well.

In Theodore Roosevelt's speech are found the precursors of social changes that occurred in the

A Bit of History

decades which immediately followed. Yet progress is not always straight forward. Roosevelt's efforts made an impact, yet income inequality still soared to another height before the stock market crashed in 1929. When the Great Depression began, inequality was once again addressed. According to Nobel Prize winning economist Paul Krugman, changes beginning in that era helped create prosperity and a broad middle class during the 1940s which lasted through the 1970s.

President Franklin Roosevelt continues to receive both praise and blame for his actions during the Great Depression even today. But it was Herbert Hoover who took the initial steps to return the economy to normalcy according to Richard Norton Smith and Timothy Walch, writing on *Archives.gov*. Hoover was a man of foresight who in 1925 as Secretary of Commerce warned President Calvin Coolidge that unrestrained speculation in the stock market could harm the economy. Claiming such speculation was "crazy and dangerous," he urged the Federal Reserve Bank to increase its discount rate on money loaned to banks for speculation. During the first summer of his presidency in 1929, Hoover, "... pressed ahead with plans for ... tax cuts graduated to favor low-income Americans. In other domestic initiatives, Hoover created the Veterans Administration and doubled the number of veterans' hospital facilities, established the antitrust division of the Justice Department to prosecute unfair competition and restraint of trade cases ..."

Just under a month after the stock market crashed in October 1929, Hoover met with major industrialists and received promises to increase employee wages from Henry Ford and railroad executives. Labor leaders also agreed to postpone their demands for higher wages. Additionally, Smith and Walch claim,

> The President ordered federal departments to

We Can Fix It

speed up construction projects. He contacted all forty-eight state governors to make a similar appeal for expanded public works. He went to Congress with a $160 million tax cut, coupled with a doubling of resources for public buildings and dams, highways, and harbors.

But the Great Depression raged on. Hoover, a private man, lacked Roosevelt's charisma—it was FDR who gained the presidency in 1933. During his 1932 campaign, Roosevelt spoke in San Francisco to members of the Commonwealth Club. The excerpts below are from that speech. To remain within the scope of this work, I've removed portions dealing with the debate between Hamilton and Jefferson, and tariffs. Some Roosevelt critics have labeled him as both a communist and a socialist. Consider these words and their context in the speech below regarding government's, "duty to protect the rights of personal freedom and of private property of all its citizens." The speech begins with a historical overview. We join it in America's second century:

> It was in the middle of the nineteenth century that a new force was released and a new dream created. The force was what is called the industrial revolution, the advance of steam and machinery and the rise of the forerunners of the modern industrial plant. The dream was the dream of an economic machine, able to raise the standard of living for everyone; to bring luxury within the reach of the humblest; to annihilate distance by steam power and later by electricity, and to release everyone from the drudgery of the heaviest manual toil. It was to be expected that this would necessarily af-

A Bit of History

fect Government. Heretofore, Government had merely been called upon to produce conditions within which people could live happily, labor peacefully, and rest secure. Now it was called upon to aid in the consummation of this new dream. There was, however, a shadow over the dream. To be made real, it required use of the talents of men of tremendous will and tremendous ambition, since by no other force could the problems of financing and engineering and new developments be brought to a consummation.

So manifest were the advantages of the machine age, however, that the United States fearlessly, cheerfully, and, I think, rightly, accepted the bitter with the sweet. It was thought that no price was too high to pay for the advantages which we could draw from a finished industrial system. The history of the last half century is accordingly in large measure a history of a group of financial Titans, whose methods were not scrutinized with too much care, and who were honored in proportion as they produced the results, irrespective of the means they used. The financiers who pushed the railroads to the Pacific were always ruthless, often wasteful, and frequently corrupt; but they did build railroads, and we have them today. ... As long as we had free land; as long as population was growing by leaps and bounds; as long as our industrial plants were insufficient to supply our own needs, society chose to give the ambitious man free play and unlimited reward provided only that he produced the economic plant so much desired. ...

We Can Fix It

Some of my friends tell me that they do not want the Government in business. With this I agree; but I wonder whether they realize the implications of the past. For while it has been American doctrine that the Government must not go into business in competition with private enterprises, still it has been traditional, particularly in Republican administrations, for business urgently to ask the Government to put at private disposal all kinds of Government assistance. The same man who tells you that he does not want to see the Government interfere in business—and he means it, and has plenty of good reasons for saying so—is the first to go to Washington and ask the Government for a prohibitory tariff on his product. When things get just bad enough, as they did two years ago, he will go with equal speed to the United States Government and ask for a loan; and the Reconstruction Finance Corporation is the outcome of it. Each group has sought protection from the Government for its own special interests, without realizing that the function of Government must be to favor no small group at the expense of its duty to protect the rights of personal freedom and of private property of all its citizens. In retrospect we can now see that the turn of the tide came with the turn of the century. We were reaching our last frontier; there was no more free land and our industrial combinations had become great uncontrolled and irresponsible units of power within the State. Clear-sighted men saw with fear the danger that opportunity would no longer be equal; that the growing corporation, like the feudal baron of old, might threaten the eco-

A Bit of History

nomic freedom of individuals to earn a living. In that hour, our antitrust laws were born. The cry was raised against the great corporations. Theodore Roosevelt, the first great Republican Progressive, fought a Presidential campaign on the issue of "trust busting" and talked freely about malefactors of great wealth. If the Government had a policy it was rather to turn the clock back, to destroy the large combinations and to return to the time when every man owned his individual small business.

This was impossible; Theodore Roosevelt, abandoning the idea of "trust busting," was forced to work out a difference between "good" trusts and "bad" trusts. The Supreme Court set forth the famous "rule of reason" by which it seems to have meant that a concentration of industrial power was permissible if the method by which it got its power, and the use it made of that power, were reasonable.

Woodrow Wilson, elected in 1912, saw the situation more clearly. Where Jefferson had feared the encroachment of political power on the lives of individuals, Wilson knew that the new power was financial. He saw, in the highly centralized economic system, the despot of the twentieth century, on whom great masses of individuals relied for their safety and their livelihood, and whose irresponsibility and greed (if they were not controlled) would reduce them to starvation and penury. The concentration of financial power had not proceeded so far in 1912 as it has today; but it had grown far enough for Mr. Wilson to realize fully its implications. It is interesting, now, to read his speeches. What is

We Can Fix It

called "radical" today (and I have reason to know whereof I speak) is mild compared to the campaign of Mr. Wilson. "No man can deny," he said, "that the lines of endeavor have more and more narrowed and stiffened; no man who knows anything about the development of industry in this country can have failed to observe that the larger kinds of credit are more and more difficult to obtain unless you obtain them upon terms of uniting your efforts with those who already control the industry of the country, and nobody can fail to observe that every man who tries to set himself up in competition with any process of manufacture which has taken place under the control of large combinations of capital will presently find himself either squeezed out or obliged to sell and allow himself to be absorbed." ...

A glance at the situation today only too clearly indicates that equality of opportunity as we have known it no longer exists. Our industrial plant is built ... there is practically no more free land. More than half of our people do not live on the farms or on lands and cannot derive a living by cultivating their own property. There is no safety valve in the form of a Western prairie to which those thrown out of work by the Eastern economic machines can go for a new start. We are not able to invite the immigration from Europe to share our endless plenty. We are now providing a drab living for our own people.

Just as freedom to farm has ceased, so also the opportunity in business has narrowed. It still is

A Bit of History

true that men can start small enterprises, trusting to native shrewdness and ability to keep abreast of competitors; but area after area has been preempted altogether by the great corporations, and even in the fields which still have no great concerns, the small man starts under a handicap. The unfeeling statistics of the past three decades show that the independent business man is running a losing race. Perhaps he is forced to the wall; perhaps he cannot command credit; perhaps he is "squeezed out," in Mr. Wilson's words, by highly organized corporate competitors, as your corner grocery man can tell you. ... Put plainly, we are steering a steady course toward economic oligarchy, if we are not there already.

Clearly, all this calls for a re-appraisal of values. A mere builder of more industrial plants, a creator of more railroad systems, an organizer of more corporations, is as likely to be a danger as a help. The day of the great promoter or the financial Titan, to whom we granted anything if only he would build, or develop, is over. Our task now is ... of meeting the problem of underconsumption, of adjusting production to consumption, of distributing wealth and products more equitably, of adapting existing economic organizations to the service of the people. The day of enlightened administration has come.

Just as in older times the central Government was first a haven of refuge, and then a threat, so now in a closer economic system the central and ambitious financial unit is no longer a servant of

We Can Fix It

national desire, but a danger. I would draw the parallel one step farther. We did not think because national Government had become a threat in the 18th century that therefore we should abandon the principle of national Government. Nor today should we abandon the principle of strong economic units called corporations, merely because their power is susceptible of easy abuse. ...

As I see it, the task of Government in its relation to business is to assist the development of an economic declaration of rights, an economic constitutional order. This is the common task of statesman and business man. It is the minimum requirement of a more permanently safe order of things.

Happily, the times indicate that to create such an order not only is the proper policy of Government, but it is the only line of safety for our economic structures as well. We know, now, that these economic units cannot exist unless prosperity is uniform, that is, unless purchasing power is well distributed throughout every group in the Nation. That is why even the most selfish of corporations for its own interest would be glad to see wages restored and unemployment ended and to bring the Western farmer back to his accustomed level of prosperity and to assure a permanent safety to both groups. That is why some enlightened industries themselves endeavor to limit the freedom of action of each man and business group within the industry in the common interest of all; why business men everywhere are asking a form of organi-

A Bit of History

zation which will bring the scheme of things into balance, even though it may in some measure qualify the freedom of action of individual units within the business. ...

I feel that we are coming to a view through the drift of our legislation and our public thinking in the past quarter century that private economic power is, to enlarge an old phrase, a public trust as well. I hold that continued enjoyment of that power by any individual or group must depend upon the fulfillment of that trust. The men who have reached the summit of American business life know this best; happily, many of these urge the binding quality of this greater social contract.

The terms of that contract are as old as the Republic, and as new as the new economic order.

Every man has a right to life; and this means that he has also a right to make a comfortable living. He may by sloth or crime decline to exercise that right; but it may not be denied him. ...

Every man has a right to his own property; which means a right to be assured, to the fullest extent attainable, in the safety of his savings. By no other means can men carry the burdens of those parts of life which, in the nature of things, afford no chance of labor; childhood, sickness, old age. In all thought of property, this right is paramount; all other property rights must yield to it. If, in accord with this principle, we must restrict the operations of the speculator, the manipulator, even the finan-

We Can Fix It

cier, I believe we must accept the restriction as needful, not to hamper individualism but to protect it. ...

> ... the responsible heads of finance and industry instead of acting each for himself, must work together to achieve the common end. They must, where necessary, sacrifice this or that private advantage; and in reciprocal self-denial must seek a general advantage. It is here that formal Government — political Government, if you chose — comes in. Whenever in the pursuit of this objective the lone wolf, the unethical competitor, the reckless promoter, the Ishmael or Insull whose hand is against every man's, declines to join in achieving an end recognized as being for the public welfare, and threatens to drag the industry back to a state of anarchy, the Government may properly be asked to apply restraint. Likewise, should the group ever use its collective power contrary to the public welfare, the Government must be swift to enter and protect the public interest.
>
> The Government should assume the function of economic regulation only as a last resort, to be tried only when private initiative, inspired by high responsibility, with such assistance and balance as Government can give, has finally failed. ...

During his presidency, Franklin Roosevelt implemented federal programs to provide work for the unemployed, regulations on banks and utilities, Social Security, and heavier taxes on the wealthy. Those in the business and financial sectors retaliated and Roosevelt failed to achieve all he intended. However, high taxation

A Bit of History

on the wealthiest Americans remained in place for decades. Taxes increased first in response to the Great Depression, later in response to World War II, and finally in order to finance the Cold War which began soon afterward. Yet, despite high top tax rates, the economy prospered. The middle class widened and grew more affluent through the 1970s.

A Middle Bulges Before Belts Tighten

I've always resented the smug statements of politicians, media commentators, corporate executives who talked of how, in America, if you worked hard you would become rich. The meaning of that was if you were poor it was because you hadn't worked hard enough. I knew this was a lie, about my father and millions of others, men and women who worked harder than anyone, harder than financiers and politicians, harder than anybody if you accept that when you work at an unpleasant job that makes it very hard work indeed. —Howard Zinn

America enjoyed a broader middle class and greater purchasing power for three decades, but these conditions ended in the 1980s. In 1973, in conjunction with the Yom Kippur War between Israel and Arab states, an embargo on oil exports was imposed by Arab states on countries which supported Israel. Gasoline prices rocketed. In some localities drivers formed lines that wrapped around the block in order to fuel their vehicles. Although the embargo ended, oil prices remained high. This led to what was called stagflation—a stagnant economy coupled to high inflation.

By the time Paul Volcker became chairman of the Federal Reserve Board in 1979, inflation was in the double digits. He began a program of raising interest rates to slow inflation. Businesses began looking for ways of cutting expenses to meet their rising costs.

We Can Fix It

These ways included what Steve Fraser called "auto-cannibalization," the practice of selling off under-performing divisions, and cutting labor costs. Labor costs were reduced in several ways including making use of cheaper overseas labor, and by weakening union bargaining strength.

From their beginning, unions and their members faced opposition, yet they managed to endure, and at times, thrive, particularly after the 1935 passage of the National Labor Relations Act (NLRA).

Prior to the passage of NLRA, laborers who wished to organize could be discouraged in a number of ways including through union infiltration by Pinkerton spies and by the employment of private militias. At times, those striking for livable wages, or decent working conditions, paid with their lives for doing so. In 1914, the Colorado National Guard fired upon and killed roughly two dozen striking coal minors along with their children and wives in Ludlow, Colorado.

The NLRA wrote into law workers' ".. right to self-organization, to form, join, or assist labor organizations, to bargain collectively through representatives of their own choosing. ..." It also prohibited a number of ways in which companies formerly discouraged employees from exercising their rights. Despite the law, some unscrupulous companies continued their previous practices.

Unions made their greatest gains during Great Depression. As a result of those gains, the working class enjoyed greater prosperity from the 1940s through the

A Middle Bulges Before Belts Tighten

1970s. However in the late 1970s union membership began to decline and has since continued doing so.

Union organizers and members have been called communists, socialists, anarchists, and agitators ever since workers began forming unions in the late 1800s. It's strange to think that workers would be called these names for asserting their right to bargain for higher wages, better working conditions, and desired benefits such as pensions and health insurance. However, name-calling has long been a tool used by those desiring to retain or increase wealth or power. Prior to and since the 2016 U.S. election, social media has swelled like an infected pustule filled with hateful names and bashed values.

Although members of labor movements have been labeled socialists and communists since those movements began, these labels took on a new significance after the Second World War. When that war concluded, the United States and the Soviet Union (USSR, Russia) emerged as the two leading world powers. In 1949, the USSR detonated its first nuclear weapon. That same year, China became a communist nation as well. Concerns about Communism led Harry S. Truman to issue a 1947 executive order requiring loyalty checks on civilians working in government agencies. Early in 1950, Alger Hiss, a suspected spy, was convicted of perjury. Not much later that year, Senator Joseph McCarthy claimed to know of 205 Communists working in the State Department. McCarthy's influence quickly rose. Soon he was conducting hearings to root out Communists. These reached a peak in 1954 before Edward R. Murrow called him out on national television and McCarthy's influence fell even more quickly than it had risen.

During the four years when McCarthy held sway, the words, "Are you now, or have you ever been, a member of the Communist party?" brought careers crashing down. Blacklisting, though everywhere denied, was particularly brutal in Hollywood. People lost jobs and were unable to obtain new ones because employers feared to hire them. The mere hint that one was a Communist or might know a Communist could endanger one's social and economic welfare. Calling union members socialists and Communists had long been a tool of industrialists. Now such name calling was disrupting lives on a grand scale. Even after the second red scare fell off in 1956, those labels stuck around for many future decades. It wasn't until 2016 that a self-identified socialist was able to gain ground as a major contender for the U.S. presidency.

The loss of fortunes following the 1929 stock market crash, along with stronger unions and higher taxes on great wealth, all played a part in the widening and greater affluence of the middle class for the decades following the Great Depression. The political climate began to change in the 1970s, however.

In their 2010 book, *Winner-Take-All Politics: How Washington Made the Rich Richer And Turned Its Back on the Middle Class,* Jacob S. Hacker and Paul

A Middle Bulges Before Belts Tighten

Pierson describe how the Great Depression brought about a change in economic thinking.

> The classical view of the market held by many economic elites at the time—and wildly held again today—distilled Adam Smith's relatively nuanced view of markets and human nature down to its free-market vapors and then mixed it with a Calvinist social Darwinism that saw economic success as a sign of superior personal character (and the reverse as a sign of individual moral failing.) [See NOTE at chapter end]

While many accepted changes begun under FDR as the new normal, others who held the classical view of the market remained in the minority during the years when the working class gained strength and the middle class broadened. The minority view that resisted social welfare and favored an unregulated market, became dormant for several decades. Republican president Dwight Eisenhower wrote these words to describe those clinging to the classical view:

> Should any political party attempt to abolish social security, unemployment insurance, and eliminate labor laws and farm programs, you would not hear of that party again in our political history. There is a tiny splinter group, of course, that believes you can do these things. Among them are H. L. Hunt (you possibly know his background), a few other Texas oil millionaires, and an occasional politician or business man from other areas. Their number is negligible and they are stupid.

Instead of Hunt, Eisenhower could as easily have named Robert Welch as an example of extreme minority views. Welch was a far right, anti-Communist. Welch believed the White House swarmed with hidden Communists and that Eisenhower himself was a Communist agent. Men of his sort, while doing their best to do their worst, still had to wait a few years before their turn at changing government arrived.

It is well known that the two major political parties in the United States have become more polarized in recent years, but that fact alone does give a complete description. The parties aren't simply more polarized: both have moved further to the right. In recent decades the popular narrative is that one party stands for a free market while the other is driven by a socialist agenda. While that myth goes far back, the reality is that for many decades the two parties promoted fairly similar agendas. If that were not the case, Eisenhower could not have written the words quoted above. In the few years between Roosevelt's and Eisenhower's presidencies, New Deal initiatives had entered the political mainstream. However, popular media largely ignores history when it isn't rewriting it. According to Hacker and Pierson,

> We know that LBJ helped usher in a period in which the federal government greatly expanded its reach not just in civil rights but in broad areas of domestic policy ranging from social programs (Medicaid and Medicare) to consumer and environmental protection. What we often forget is that, in all these areas and more, Washington remained on course following the 'crucible' elections of 1968 and 1972.

Their story continues,

> Nixon, not Johnson, signed into law the huge extensions of national regulatory policy that marked

A Middle Bulges Before Belts Tighten

this period, creating the Environmental Protection Agency (1970), the Occupational Safety and Health Administration (1970), the National Traffic Safety Commission (1972), and the Mine Safety and Health Administration (1973). And while Nixon had been forced out of office by the time the massive Employee Retirement Income Security Act (1974) made it through Congress, his Successor, Gerald Ford, signed the bill ...

This onslaught of occupational and environmental regulations alarmed the business community:

> Now companies across a wide range of sectors faced a common threat: increasingly powerful regulatory agencies overseeing their treatment of the environment, workers, and consumers. Individual firms had little chance of fending off such broad initiatives on their own; to craft an appropriately broad political defense, they needed organization.

Some of that organization was supplied by members of the far right. Today that faction owns much of the political dialog. The business community organized effectively and made its voice heard:

> By 1978, at a time of unified Democratic control of the House, Senate, and White House, the precursors of the Reagan revolution were already visible. Congress passed a tax bill whose signature provision was a deep cut in the capital gains tax—a change that would largely benefit the wealthy. This followed hard on the heels of a decision to sharply raise payroll taxes, the most regressive federal levy. ... The United States began its long, dramatic move

We Can Fix It

away from the established practice of using taxes as an instrument for tempering market-generated inequalities associated with the outsized earnings of those at the top.

Between 1976 and mid-1980, corporate Political Action Committees (PACs) increased more than fourfold, from fewer than 300 to more than 1,200. The 1973 oil embargo brought on a decade of rising fuel prices. When these increase, prices for whatever requires transportation also increase. Computers to some extent have lowered the costs of delivering goods such as eBooks, yet even now nearly all goods are affected by transportation costs, often at multiple stages in their creation.

In the 1970s the United States experienced a period of economic stagnation coupled with inflation—a phenomena named stagflation. As businesses looked to cut costs, labor was one place ripe for cost cutting. Union strength fell off dramatically. At their height, unions exerted a strong political force, educating workers on relevant issues and encouraging them to vote. According to Hacker and Pierson, for example, labor union leadership provided the necessary momentum to boost the Civil Rights Act across the finish line. Just as labor unions were losing their voices, free market advocates were gaining theirs.

Eisenhower's presidency began in the final days of McCarthyism and continued into early 1961. Although McCarthy's influence declined, some people retained their anti-communist fervor. One of these, retired industrialist Robert Welch, founded the John Birch Society (JBS) in 1958, writes Alvin Felzenberg in *Nationalreview.com*. Several former leaders of the National Association of Manufacturers were at its first meeting. Welch argued that communists had deeply penetrated the United States. President Eisenhower

A Middle Bulges Before Belts Tighten

himself had fallen under their influence. National Review founder, William F. Buckley, Jr., and Robert Welch initially lent each other support. However, Buckley later distanced himself from Welch. After the two parted ways, Buckley accused Welch of inferring "subjective intention from objective consequences," for example, assuming that public policies which went wrong had been deliberately designed to do so.

Barry Goldwater's defeat in the 1964 presidential race was largely due to the opposing party successfully arguing that Goldwater's views were dangerously far to the right. It probably didn't help that the JBS had lent its support to his candidacy. Goldwater, however, was no fan of Welch. Goldwater, in fact, once advised Welch to burn every copy of the book Welch had written.

Nor were Goldwater and Buckley alone in viewing Welch and the JBS as advocating extreme views. Both Bob Dylan and the Chad Mitchell Trio recorded songs that mocked the JBS.

One founding member of the JBS was an industrialist named Fred Koch. Fred fathered four sons. Of these, two, Charles and David, have played a strong part in shifting America to the right. In 1976 Charles organized a conference at which he presented a paper. In her book, *Dark Money: The Hidden History of the Billionaires Behind the Rise of the Radical Right,* Jane Mayer reports that Charles Koch's paper:

> ... methodically analyzed the strengths and weaknesses of a group he knew intimately, the John Birch Society, as a model for their future enterprise. His assessment was clear-eyed and businesslike. He pointed out that despite the fringe group's shortcomings, it boasted 90,000 members, 240 paid staffers, and a $7 million annual budget. While these numbers were impressive, he faulted

We Can Fix It

the John Birch Society's obsession with conspiracies, as well as the unchecked cult of personality that Welch had built up. He noted that Welch's ownership of the organization's stock had centralized control in his hands, making him impervious to constructive criticism. (Interestingly, Charles would go on to issue stock in his own nonprofit think tank, the Cato Institute, in much the same way.) But he also found much to admire. In particular, he argued in favor of copying the John Birch Society's secrecy.

The Kochs, Mayer claims,

> ... sought ways to steer American politics hard to the right without having to win the popular vote, they got valuable reinforcement from a small cadre of like-minded wealthy conservative families who were harnessing their own corporate fortunes toward the same end. Philanthropy, with its guarantees of anonymity, became their chosen instrument. But their goal was patently political: to undo not just Lyndon Johnson's Great Society and Franklin Roosevelt's New Deal but Teddy Roosevelt's Progressive Era, too. In taking on this daunting task, they were in many cases refighting battles that had been lost by their fathers.

As the first volleys were fired, few saw them coming. The Kochs and their allies had the advantage of surprise in the class war they'd begun. Stealth, too, offered advantages. Money moved from "private foundations and trusts" into newly formed political think tanks. By carefully choosing their funding methods, the super wealthy avoided close scrutiny. According to Mayer,

A Middle Bulges Before Belts Tighten

Their grants were soon mixed with those from corporate donors, who cautiously followed the families' bold lead. Unlike other forms of paid political influence, much of this money was never revealed. Gifts to nonprofit groups could be concealed from the public.

Through examining the papers of Clare Boothe Luce, the names of some of the early sponsors of the Heritage Foundation were revealed. They included,

> ... Amoco, Amway, Boeing, Chase Manhattan Bank, Chevron, Dow Chemical, Exxon, General Electric, General Motors, Mesa Petroleum, Mobil Oil, Pfizer, Philip Morris, Procter & Gamble, R. J. Reynolds, Searle, Sears, Roebuck, SmithKline Beckman, Union Carbide, and Union Pacific ...

Note how many of those names are of chemical and petroleum companies—companies whose activities have been linked to causing environmental damage and contributing to climate change.

For men like Charles Koch, it's all about money. Influencing public policy by funding think tanks is a small price to pay for avoiding social responsibility. According to a 2014 Rolling Stone article by Tim Dickinson, Koch Industries, "... ranks 13th in the nation for toxic air pollution. Koch's climate pollution, meanwhile, outpaces oil giants including Valero, Chevron and Shell." But Koch Industries doesn't just make the environment dirty, it plays dirty as well. In 1996 a pre-college teen smelled gas and became ill. Since her parents couldn't afford a phone, she and her friend drove off to find help. When their truck stalled out and they attempted to restart it, a spark ignited the butane-filled creek bed that crossed their driveway. The truck and its teenage occupants were swallowed in flames. The leaked butane came from an idled pipeline that had recently been put back in service. During its inspection, 538 flaws were found in the pipeline. Only 80 of these were then repaired. In order to comply with a directive from Charles, Koch Industries managers cut costs by skimping on necessary repairs. According to Dickinson, during subsequent testimony, Kenoth Whitstine, a former manager, said, "Koch Industries has a philosophy that profits are above everything else." When a man is more interested in being wealthy than in being neighborly, he knows that it's cheaper to pay fines than to obey regulations.

Writing on *Washingtonpost.com* on September 5, 2017, Robert O'Harrow Jr. states that when the president announced his decision on June 1, 2017 to withdraw from the Paris Climate Accord, Myron Ebell was among the onlookers in the White House Rose Garden. As leader of the Cooler Heads Coalition. Ebell had spent 20 years denying climate change. Along the way his coalition had acquired millions in donations from nonprofit foundations controlled by wealthy families including the Kochs and others. ExxonMobil, long-time denier of climate change, was also among the donors. Ebell had served his funders well. They, in turn, enriched themselves at government expense, paying to deny climate change through charitable donations with money that would otherwise have been taxed.

Charles Koch, who advocates for smaller government and fewer regulations, achieves both through organizations like the Cooler Heads Coalition. His deductible charitable contributions deprive government of tax revenue, essentially making government smaller or driving it deeper into debt. At the same time, he shields his business interests from undesired regulations by using the tax code to make contributions. While claiming to be against regulations, men like Koch are able to use favorable regulations

A Middle Bulges Before Belts Tighten

within the tax code to fund self-serving projects. When they claim to favor unregulated markets, they fool themselves, just as they fool the public. They aren't against all regulations—they're only against the regulations they don't like.

Today's wealthy players make the Robber Barons of the Gilded Age look like amateurs. Claiming that an unregulated market was at the heart of a strong United States, they've grabbed hold of the nation's dialog on economic policy while growing their wealth and keeping wages stagnant for most other Americans.

The middle class has shrunk since the 1980s. Today's income inequality looks much as it did in 1929 just before the stock market crashed. Further, income inequality appears to be growing both in the United States and worldwide. In January 2017, *Oxfam.org* reported that just eight individuals hold as much wealth as 50 percent of humanity. In 2010, 388 people owned half the world's wealth, notes Walter Scheidel in his book, *The Great Leveler : Violence and the History of Inequality from the Stone Age to the Twenty-first Century*. Between 2010 and 2017 half the world's wealth fell into 380 fewer pairs of hands.

What does income inequality look like within the United States? Using the most recent Federal Reserve data (2016), Jacobin found that 77 percent of the nation's private wealth can be found among its top 10 percent. The top one percent alone holds 38.5 percent of this wealth. Using the same data, DQYDT supplied these numbers:

We Can Fix It

Net worth percentile rank and dollars owned

10.0% — ($962) Assumed to be in debt
20.0% — $4,798
30.0% — $18,753
40.0% — $49,132
50.0% — $97,225 Net wealth for half of Americans
60.0% — $169,550
70.0% — $279,594
80.0% — $499,263
90.0% — $1,182,390
95.0% — $2,377,985
96.0% — $2,798,189
97.0% — $3,703,775
98.0% — $5,816,220 For 2017, estates are taxed above $5.49 million
99.0% — $10,374,030 In 2018, estates become taxable when over $11.2 million
99.5% — $16,115,373
99.9% — $43,090,281 A rounded 10% of Charles Koch's wealth

Our current extreme income inequality comes paired with other threats. If we are to deal effectively with climate change, we must do so quickly. Delay will make its effects worse and those effects could last centuries. Some would prevent us from repairing our earth. They're willing to use their wealth to hamper progress even though they're hurting their own decedents as well as all of humanity. This I believe: Even if climate change were a myth, income inequality urgently needs to be reduced. More than one in eight Americans now live in poverty. Others are only a

A Middle Bulges Before Belts Tighten

paycheck or two away from doing so. And for others still, a single health care emergency could drive them into poverty. This alone threatens our social framework. But there's another rising threat—robots are coming and they want your job.

[NOTE: Although Hacker and Pierson don't elaborate on the phrase, "Calvinist social Darwinism," they may in part be referring to concepts discussed by sociologist, Max Weber in his, "The Protestant Ethic and the Spirit of Capitalism." Published in two parts in 1904 and 1905, Weber's thesis is that several Protestant denominations, notably Calvinism, influenced how Capitalism developed into its current form. As believers in predestination, Protestants had no assurance of salvation, as did Catholics through priestly absolution. Protestants sought assurance of salvation through frugality, following a calling, and performing works that glorified God. A thriving business and the accumulation of capital could be interpreted as a sign that one was glorifying God, and was one of the elect who would be saved. Such a belief justified Capitalist activity. Glorifying God through works was considered virtuous. This allowed the prosperous to view themselves as righteous, and to view the poor as ungodly. Weber notes that in contemporary Germany belief in God had nearly disappeared, while the Protestant Ethic continued to justify Capitalism.

Weber's idea of the Protestant Ethic remains controversial. I've addressed it briefly because it neatly explains such things as the (alleged) frugality of New England Yankees.

Following Darwin's release of *On the Origin of Species* in 1859, some clerics sought to broaden their religious conceptions to include evolution. While they treated Christianity figuratively, others treated it literally. Today, those who view Christianity literally are among the most socially vocal. During the 1880s the concept of social Darwinism sprang up. The idea here is that the fittest survive and thrive, while the unfit do not. Social Darwinism is a good way to blame the poor for their poverty, and oddly remains so along with variations, even among those Christians who deny evolution.]

The Robots Are Coming

Let us remember that the automatic machine is the precise economic equivalent of slave labor. Any labor which competes with slave labor must accept the economic consequences of slave labor. —Norbert Wiener

What's wrong with robots? In May 2017, Jen Deaderick writing for The NBER Digest on *Nber.org* reported,

> Since at least the start of the Industrial Revolution, economists and policy makers have pondered how relentless technological advances might impact labor markets. John Maynard Keynes warned in 1929 of coming "technological unemployment" and Wassily Leontief predicted several decades later that 'labor will become less and less important.' In recent years, a range of studies has estimated that nearly half of all U.S. workers' jobs will be at risk of being automated over the next two decades, and noted that this risk extends beyond laborers to include many white-collar occupations with substantial routine components.

Let's repeat that, "nearly half." That's a lot of jobs. But that estimate may not go far enough. The article draws its conclusions from a study using a precise definition of robots. That is, "the International Federation of Robotics (IFR) definition of robots as autonomous, reprogrammable, multipurpose machines; this excludes single-purpose automated machinery and artificial intelligence technologies." This definition has its limits. Machinery implies moving parts. But if you take away its cooling fans and spinning storage drives, a computer only has those moving parts which are used for external input, i.e. mice and keyboards.

Kevin Drum uses a looser definition of robots in his 2017 *Mother Jones* article, "You Will Lose Your Job to a Robot." He includes artificial intelligence (AI) as a component of robotics. It's difficult to assess the effects of AI because it hasn't yet arrived. Instead, what we have are programs that come ever closer to appearing intelligent. Since AI is developing incrementally, it's hard to see the finish line. Drum believes we'll see significant effects from this emerging technology within ten years. The World Economic Forum, he reports, predicts that wealthy countries will lose five million jobs to robots during the next three years. And Kai-Fu Lee, an executive who once worked at Google and Microsoft, claims that half of the world's jobs will be performed with AI in only ten years time. Between robots that are programmable, but not very smart, and devices that act smart, but don't move very much, the threat is huge.

Drum offers the usual objection to emerging technology in order to refute it: "… waves of automation—steam engines, electricity, computers—always lead to predictions of mass unemployment. Instead they just make us more efficient. The AI revolution will be no different." But then he reminds us that when machinery entered the picture, people "really did lose their livelihoods. This caused massive social upheaval for decades until the entire economy adapted to the machine age." When that happened, those who once did the work of machines now tended them. However, "When robots become as smart and capable as human beings, there will be nothing left for people to do because machines will be both stronger and smarter than humans."

The Robots Are Coming

Drum describes three potential steps societies might take as the robots advance upon us. The first is merely an expansion of entitlements such as Unemployment Insurance and Medicaid. In this stage, denial will prevail. People will be assisted with the expectation that they seek work—that is, jobs that have vanished and won't return. His other two steps are variations on Universal Basic Income.

I have problems believing that there will ever be Universal Basic Income in the United States. My first doubt is this—Belgium, Canada, Iceland, Japan, Portugal, Sweden, and the United Kingdom, all have Universal Healthcare—and that's just a partial list. The United States does not have Universal Healthcare and never will unless its political environment changes drastically. If our country refuses to implement Universal Healthcare, as a fair number of other advanced nations have done, why should we assume that Universal Basic Income will be implemented as people begin losing jobs to robots? The 2017 Tax Cuts and Jobs Act largely benefits the wealthy while increasing the national debt. Some speculate that debt will become an issue soon and that it will be addressed by reducing payments to Medicaid and Medicare, programs which benefit the poor, disabled, and elderly. Unless the political focus moves away from satisfying rich men's greed to meeting common men's needs, I don't envision Universal Basic Income gaining any traction in this country.

Later I'll discuss how the super-wealthy have gained control of both our economy and our politics. They would surely oppose Universal Basic Income just as they oppose Universal Healthcare. Opposition to Universal Basic Income will be called a free handout to those too lazy to work. Currently many regard Medicaid, Medicare, and Social Security as forms of socialism—and those programs are already established.

We Can Fix It

Universal Healthcare is regarded as a more extreme form of socialism. This shouldn't be the case. Universal Healthcare works well in a number of capitalist countries. Socialism became a scary word during the Cold War, but there's no reason for it to be scary now. Social entitlement programs have operated for decades without destroying capitalism. Yet outworn ideas, like outworn clothes, are frequently patched and stubbornly retained when they should be tossed out.

Another reason I'm dubious about Universal Basic Income is because I believe people need jobs, or callings, lest they feel obsolete and useless. By "job" what I mean is a meaningful occupation, not the sort of meaningless drudgery that makes one eager to get home and numb oneself in some manner before the next work shift begins.

In his 2016 book, *Four Futures: Visions of the World After Capitalism*, Peter Frase examines the possible effects of several current trends. Examining unemployment, Frase reports a study that found peoples' self-esteem improved when they considered their status to be retired rather than unemployed. Retirement carries no social stigma. It implies spending one's time engaging in enjoyable and meaningful activities. Unemployment does carry a social stigma however. Being unemployed can leave one feeling that one is no longer useful—that one is a failure, one of society's rejects. People need meaning and respect in their lives, and that generally comes through work. If a robotic society is to be a satisfactory one, people will need to find new meanings in their lives.

Frase addresses two looming problems—climate change and the advance of robotics. While robotics could accelerate productivity, climate change could bring famine. Both could increase social disruption. Although Frase writes from a socialist perspective, that bias doesn't cripple his objectivity. Two of his futures

The Robots Are Coming

are of abundance: one describes a hierarchal society, the other a more egalitarian society. Frase's other two futures also contrast hierarchy and equality, except in these scarcity prevails. Since my concern is with preserving capitalism, and since capitalism implies social hierarchy, I only consider two of Frase's futures. Neither appear to turn out well.

Frase reports that the term "rentier" came into being in nineteenth century France to describe holders of government bonds. This is the origin of the economist's term, rent seeking. The term describes any revenue gained through ownership of scarce resources. For example, since land is limited, if you own some land you can collect rent from it. However, if you're the first to bring a new innovation to market, you can also gain rents during the period prior to other businesses making use of that innovation. Copyright and patent rent seeking currently limit competition and startup opportunities in the technology industry. In the case of robotics and computer software, patents and copyrights prevent others from making use of your assets without paying their rental fees. Rents are a good means of gaining revenue without having to actively supply labor or pay for ongoing costs.

In his chapter on Rentism, Frase discusses a future in which those who own the robots and the software that drives them will control society's major assets. Rentism might look something like this:

> Star Trek provides a fable of an egalitarian, post-scarcity society. But what does that look like without the egalitarianism? In other words, given the material abundance made possible by the replicator, how would it be possible to maintain a system based on money, profit, and class power?
>
> Economists like to say that capitalist market econ-

We Can Fix It

omies work optimally when they are used to allocate scarce goods. So how to maintain capitalism in a world were scarcity can be largely overcome? This requires a kind of antithesis of the Star Trek universe, which takes the same technical preconditions and casts them in a different set of social relations.

As noted above, intellectual property differs from other property because it grants rights not just over concrete objects but over patterns and all copies and uses of those patterns. And the entire infrastructure of Star Trek is based on patterns that are fed into the replicator and used as the basis for fabricating a physical object, just as a blueprint provides the guidelines for building a house.

This is the quality of intellectual property law that provides an economic foundation for anti–Star Trek: the ability to tell others how to use copies of an idea or pattern that you "own." So imagine that unlike Star Trek, we don't all have access to our own replicators. And that in order to get access to a replicator, you would have to buy one from a company that licenses you the right to use it. You can't get someone to give you a replicator or make one with their replicator, because that would violate their license and get them in legal trouble. What's more, every time you make something with the replicator, you also need to pay a licensing fee to whoever owns the rights to that particular thing. Captain Jean-Luc Picard customarily walks to the replicator and requests "tea, Earl Grey, hot." But his anti–Star Trek counterpart would have to pay

The Robots Are Coming

the company that has copyrighted the replicator pattern for hot Earl Grey tea.

    What jobs would be available in a society like this? There would of course be jobs for those who create the ideas that become copyrighted. There would also be plenty of work for lawyers who would spend their time trying to punish infringements of copyrights and patents. Much effort would also go into advertising the benefits that make one product superior to a similar product. And then there would be policing jobs to prevent the less fortunate from failing to pay rent on the intellectual property of the wealthy. Eventually, as all the wealth ended up in the hands of an elite few, the government might have to step in with artificial solutions to keep the economy running. And those solutions would require frequent and fine tuning to keep the economy balanced between, "… ongoing stagnation and periodic economic crisis. …"
    The frequent tuning such an economy would require is reminiscent of the planned economy of the former Soviet Union. There, government planning created inefficiencies and shortages. People spent hours in lines just to acquire basic goods. I believe similar problems would arise once the government begins trying to balance out a Rentist economy. Every new innovation will disrupt the status quo and therefore innovation will be discouraged. What would begin as a world of ample goods and toys would end in a dull and meaningless society.
    If such a future weren't bad enough, Frase offers a grimmer one he calls Exterminism. Unlike Rentism, in which abundance must be distributed in a hierarchical society, Exterminism is a future in which the social hierarchy exists in the world of scarcity rather than abundance. Frase uses the movie *Elysium* to illustrate such a society. In this movie the poor living on a

We Can Fix It

poisoned earth are denied the luxuries and the good healthcare that are available to the elites living in Elysium.

That movie implies a happy ending, but what if the resources don't exist to supply such an ending? Frase asks,

> What if we arrive in a future that no longer requires the mass proletariat's labor in production but is unable to provide everyone with an arbitrarily high standard of consumption? If we arrive in that world as an egalitarian society, our system will resemble the socialist regime of shared conservation described in the previous section. But if, instead, we remain a society polarized between a privileged elite and a downtrodden mass, then the most plausible trajectory leads to something much darker. The rich will sit secure in the knowledge that their replicators and robots can provide for their every need. What of the rest of us?

When the poor become "merely a danger and an inconvenience," exterminating them may become a viable option. I know this sounds like something a paranoid conspiracy theorist might think up, but it's not without precedent in recent history. In 1942 Germany, a small group held a conference in order to discuss the "Jewish Question," By the time the meeting concluded they had contrived the "final solution." Extermination camps were then built for the sole purpose of destroying Jewish lives.

Flash forward to 1975 Cambodia. The Khmer Rouge took control of the government and began killing the country's people. By the time they were defeated, an estimated quarter of the population had been put to death either directly or through starvation. Again, in

The Robots Are Coming

1994 a round of genocide began when Hutu extremists took control during the power vacuum following the downing of the Rwandan president's plane. Radio broadcasters urged Hutus to kill their Tutsi co-countrymen, and they did as they were urged. There have been other genocides, but three examples are sufficient.

It needn't be so dramatic or happen all at once. It could begin as in the movie, *Elysium,* with the elite removing themselves from those places where the rabble dwell. In fact, they are already doing so by moving into gated communities. Frase considers, "... Cartier jewelry executive Johann Rupert, who told a 2015 *Financial Times* conference that the prospect of an insurgency among the poor is 'what keeps me awake at night.'"

It's a problem. What are the well-off to do about the impoverished? Before the Nazis began exterminating Jews, they first incarcerated them beginning in 1933. It took a few years for them to realize that a final solution was called for. One would think that a people who lived through the Holocaust would be too sensitive to ever treat another people as they themselves were treated. Many are that sensitive, but not all. You may think me tactless for including this next quote from Frase's book. Regardless, here it is:

> At one time, Israel heavily depended on cheap Palestinian labor. But as political economist Adam Hanieh has demonstrated, since the late 1990s these workers have been displaced by migrant laborers from Asia and Eastern Europe. Having thus rendered Palestinians superfluous as workers, Israel is able to give free reign to the more fanatical aspects of Zionism's settler-colonial project. In its 2014 assault on the Gaza Strip, the government

We Can Fix It

> made claims of "self-defense" that were almost laughably perfunctory, even as they bombed hospitals, schools, and power plants, indiscriminately killing men, women, and children alike and leveling much of the housing stock. Open calls for genocide came from members of the Israeli parliament; one, Ayelet Shaked, proclaimed that "the entire Palestinian people is the enemy." On this basis she justified the destruction of Gaza as a whole, "including its elderly and its women, its cities and its villages, its property and its infrastructure."

Ayelet Shaked's views may not be those of a typical Israeli. None-the-less, the argument could be made that the impoverished and poorly educated are warehoused in prisons right here at home. Frase puts it this way, "The American prison system has long been a way to control the unemployed who get locked away inside while buying off those who remain on the outside." The system serves multiple purposes—it provides profits for those who build and run privatized prisons while bringing jobs to more rural areas.

> The resulting explosion in prison construction, meanwhile, provides jobs in rural areas of the state with depressed economies. With agricultural work automated or shifted to ultra-low-wage migrant labor, and manufacturing jobs lost to deindustrialization, prison work has become among the last remaining well-paid labor in these places.

I imagine most readers are thinking that an Exterminism future could never occur in the United States. Yet few can deny that the political and social mood in our country today is vastly different from what it was as recently as two years ago. Exterminism may

The Robots Are Coming

not be as far-fetched as it seems. Regardless of whether the climate may be changing, the human population is more numerous than it has ever been, and this alone puts a strain on the environment. In many parts of the world water is scarce and huge swaths of once-green land are becoming desert. Here in the United States the Ogallala Aquifer, with portions beneath eight states, is in danger of running dry. That water took centuries to get there. It can't be replaced. The UN refugee agency reports on *Unhcr.org* that millions of people are living in refugee camps outside the United States. The Great Wall didn't save China from invasion. A Mexican border wall won't work here either. If a flood is strong enough, the dam will break. If we're to avoid Exterminism, or other dystopias in our future, we've got to find solutions now.

The Silenced Majority

But the meek shall inherit the earth; and shall delight themselves in the abundance of peace.
—Psalm 37:11

When more voices have opportunities to be heard, common sense suggests that more ideas will be generated. For this reason discussion is often encouraged in schools and workplaces. In the political realm, however, discussion is being discouraged. Some voices are shouting while others barely whisper. This isn't because soft-spoken people need to be louder—it's because those doing the shouting are doing it with money, not their voices. The soft-spoken lack the money to buy advertising, pay for lobbyists, fund think tanks, and hire paid experts to bend politicians' ears.

Under U.S. law, corporations are in many ways considered artificial persons which share most of the rights of real persons. Corporate personhood is a legal fiction that treats corporations as if they were persons. This treatment has many advantages and our economy depends upon such a fiction. The creation of corporate charters allowed individuals to collectively invest money while limiting their personal liabilities if those investments soured.

In 2014, Nina Totenberg interviewed John Coffee for NPR. According to Coffee, the Catholic Church may have been the first organization permitted, like corporations, to trade property as individuals do. Initially governments granted a limited number of corporate charters in order to further various social ends, but today they are ubiquitous. The problem with corporate personhood is that, while society has changed, legal thinking remains stuck in the past.

In its 2010 ruling, in the case of *Citizens United v. FEC*, the Supreme Court overruled laws that prohibited corporations from airing political advertisements. Although corporations cannot work directly with political campaigns, they can none-the-less influence voter's views through advertising. With this Supreme Court ruling, the concept of corporate personhood now includes another basic right, that of free speech. Writing for *Scotusblog.com,* Lisa McElroy reports that only five of the nine Supreme Court Justices agreed with the ruling. The remaining four Justices, "... voiced the concern that allowing unfettered spending by rich corporations will allow those corporations to influence the outcome of elections in sweeping ways. They also explained that corporations are not human beings and should not have the same free speech rights that humans do."

Critics of the decision argue that the Supreme Court equates free spending with free speech. Corporations, too, apparently agree with the Supreme Court. The more they spend, the more freely they speak. Since the Supreme Court decision, corporate election contributions have seen huge increases. Ellen L. Weintraub, voicing her opinion in 2016 on *Nytimes.com*, considers Justice Kennedy's use of the

The Silenced Majority

words, "associations of citizens" when considering corporate rights to political expression. Noting that non-citizens cannot donate to American elections, she questions the rights of non-citizen shareholders in voicing their opinions through corporate advertising. Did the Supreme Court inadvertently open up a loophole through which foreign interests can pour their money?

A traditional legal assumption regarding corporate personhood is that a corporation's constituents all share a consensual set of beliefs. Workers are deprived of agency by assuming that they share their employer's ideals. They could hate their employer's ideas, but instead work there due to economic need.

In her 2016 book, Jane Mayer reports that in the early 1970s wealthy donors began to fund think tanks and other recipients of what McGeorge Bundy calls "advocacy philanthropy." Some of these donors resented the new environmental regulations they were required to follow.

When the state of Virginia confronted Olin Corporation with stricter environmental regulations, it responded that it wouldn't be able to comply. Instead, claiming additional other reasons, it decided to close its Saltville facility. It then, "… demolished its factory and sold most of its Saltville real estate back to local residents but found no takers for its mercury waste 'muck' pond." Mayer quotes Harry Haynes, son of a former Olin employee,

We Can Fix It

'We all played with the mercury as children,' he recalls. 'Daddy brought it home from the chemical plant. You'd drop it on the floor, and it would explode into a zillion little bits, and then sweep it together and it would clump back together again.' The company issued gas masks to workers because of the pervasive chemical vapors, but, another resident recalled, 'no one wore them.'

Mayer quotes Shirley "Sissy" Bailey, another Saltville resident:

'To this day, that muck pond is still there, and you can still see clumps of mercury along the river. The drinking water is so full of lead and mercury it isn't fit for a dog to drink.' She says she "lived" the history, ran as a kid on riverbanks so poisoned no grass grew. The air often smelled of chlorine and other chemicals. 'The Olin Company was dirty and treated the people bad, not like people,' she says. 'Most of the workers were poorly educated, and they led them around like sheep.'

I wonder if the workers at Olin's Saltville plant shared the same ideals as their employer. Justice Kennedy's argument may occasionally apply to some workers, but I can't believe that corporations are invariably "associations of citizens."

That argument is even less valid in contemporary America. In his book, *Saving Capitalism: For the many, not the few,* Robert B. Reich discusses stakeholder capitalism versus shareholder capitalism. During the middle of the twentieth century American corporations felt obligated to all their stakeholders—stockholders, employees, and consumers. In such a corporate environment, unions, decent benefits, and

The Silenced Majority

livable wages could thrive. Corporations could hold their heads up in civic pride. Reich states,

> ... in the first three decades following World War II, corporate managers saw their job as balancing the claims of investors, employees, consumers, and the public at large. The large corporation was in fact 'owned' by everyone with a stake in how it performed." But the mood changed during the 1980s as raiders attempted to justify corporate takeovers. Some economists agreed with them, claiming that stakeholder capitalism was inefficient. "They argued that under the pressure of shareholders, corporations move economic resources to where they are most productive and thereby enable the entire economy to grow faster.

He then adds,

> Yet when you take a hard look at the consequences of shareholder capitalism that took root in the 1980s—a legacy that includes flat or declining wages for most Americans, along with growing economic insecurity, outsourced jobs, abandoned communities, CEO pay that his soared into the stratosphere, a myopic focus on quarterly earnings, and a financial sector akin to a casino whose near failure in 2008 imposed collateral damage on most Americans—you might have some doubts about how well shareholder capitalism has worked in practice.

Returning to Olin Corporation and its leadership, Mayer writes,

> It was, however, against a backdrop of serious

clashes with the increasingly robust regulatory state that John Olin directed his lawyer to enlist his fortune in the battle to defend corporate America. As he put it, "My greatest ambition now is to see free enterprise reestablished in this country. Business and the public must be awakened to the creeping stranglehold that socialism has gained here since World War II."

Is there a connection between environmental regulations and socialism? Some would say so. These are the "advocacy philanthropists" who favor a self-regulating free market otherwise known as a laissez faire economic system—one which is guided by an "invisible hand." Early economist Adam Smith is credited with coining the term "invisible hand," yet he used it sparingly and not entirely in the context in which it is currently used. Writing in 2001 on *Nytimes.com*, Alan B. Krueger presents a broader view of Adam Smith. He writes that while Smith found value in free trade and self-interest, he also cared about those who were property-less. He writes that,

> Smith passionately argued, 'When the regulation, therefore, is in support of the workman, it is always just and equitable; but it is sometimes otherwise when in favour of the masters.' He saw a tacit conspiracy on the part of employers 'always and everywhere' to keep wages as low as possible.

In the view of the "advocacy philanthropists," however, workers who seek fair wages are socialists and a free market guided by an invisible hand keeps the economy purring. Regulations, such as those aimed at keeping air and water clean, prevent the invisible hand from doing its job.

The Silenced Majority

Reich challenges the claim that there ever has been, or ever can be, an unregulated market guided by an invisible hand:

> Markets depend for their very existence on rules governing property (what can be owned), monopoly (what degree of market power is permissible), contracts (what can be exchanged and under what terms), bankruptcy (what happens when purchasers can't pay up), and how all this is enforced.

Reich then elaborates,

> [A] market—any market—requires that government make and enforce the rules of the game. In most modern democracies, such roles emanate from legislatures, administrative agencies, and courts. Government doesn't 'intrude' on the 'free market.' It creates the market.

Jane Mayer describes the new "advocacy philanthropists" in great depth. She writes of how billionaires led by Charles and David Koch, two of the four brothers, have used their own money and that of other wealthy "investors" to influence the political dialog prevalent in the United States. Writing of a 2009 meeting hosted by the Kochs, she describes the donors in attendance.

> Most, like the Kochs, were businessmen with vast personal fortunes that placed them not just in the top 1 percent of the nation's wealthiest citizens but in a more rarefied group, the top 0.1 percent or higher. By most standards, they were extraordinarily successful. But for this cohort, Obama's election represented a galling setback. During the

previous eight years of Republican rule, this conservative corporate elite had consolidated its power, amassing enormous sway over the U.S. government's regulatory and tax laws. Some in this group faulted President Bush for not having been conservative enough. But having molded policy to serve their interests during the Bush years, many members of this caste had accumulated phenomenal wealth and regarded the newly elected Democratic president as a direct threat to all they had gained.

She describes the Kochs as being, "among a small, rarefied group of hugely wealthy, archconservative families that for decades poured money, often with little public disclosure, into influencing how Americans thought and voted." They used several methods:

> [T]hey subsidized networks of seemingly unconnected think tanks and academic programs and spawned advocacy groups to make their arguments in the national political debate. They hired lobbyists to push their interests in Congress and operatives to create synthetic grassroots groups to give their movement political momentum on the ground. In addition, they financed legal groups and judicial junkets to press their cases in the courts. Eventually, they added to this a private political machine that rivaled and threatened to subsume, the Republican Party much of this activism was cloaked in secrecy and presented as philanthropy, leaving almost no money trail that the public could trace.

The Silenced Majority

Spending to influence political discourse began long before the Supreme Court decided *Citizens United v. FEC*. The Court's decision made such spending far easier however. Spending that had caused a roar now causes hearing loss. It's established that the Russians tried to influence the 2016 U.S. election with fake news advertising. Additionally, America now has a leader that fact checkers claim lied hundreds of times since taking office. That leader complains the loudest about fake news. By doing so he attempts to discredit those who criticize him. This may fool some of the people but it makes others angry and uncertain. Behind the scenes, those with big bucks continue to steer social policy.

Dissatisfied Americans are raising their voices on social media. But civil discourse is becoming increasingly scarce on social media. It's become an undisciplined schoolyard, complete with bullies, rude comments, and name-calling. Meanwhile, politicians do their listening elsewhere, in offices where they greet and meet with lobbyists and wealthy donors. The average working person is ignored while the elite provide the framework, rules, and direction of political and social policy discussion. Since only the wealthiest are heard, fewer fresh ideas are generated and discussed. Without a broader range of American viewpoints reaching politicians' ears, critical issues like climate change, an automated future, and a crumbling infrastructure don't get addressed.

What does get addressed? Only what those with the money want to address. Reich reports:

> ... according to a 2014 pew research poll, a large majority of Americans, regardless of party, were worried about jobs. Yet when political scientists Benjamin Page and Larry Bartels surveyed Chicagoans with an average net worth of 14 million, they found their biggest concerns were either the budget

deficit or excessive government spending, ranking these as priorities three times as often as they did unemployment. And—no surprise—these wealthy individuals were also far less willing than other Americans to curb deficits by raising taxes on high-income people and more willing to cut Social Security and Medicare. They also opposed initiatives most other Americans favored, such as increasing spending on schools and raising the minimum wage.

Further, two thirds of these wealthy respondents had made substantial political contributions within the last year's time. If this is what happens in Chicago, imagine what happens nationwide.

To what degree do the interests of the wealthy shape the public policy agenda? Sitaraman cites a major study by Martin Gilens. He reports that Gilens

> ... has conducted the most comprehensive study of the relationship between wealth and political influence, based on an analysis of public policy over two decades. He finds the government policy across all policy areas reflects the policy preferences of the affluent and that the views of the poor and the middle class have no effect on outcomes. "What that means is that when the poor and the middle class—when 70 percent of the people—disagree with the views of the richest 10 percent, their views have no effect on public policy outcomes. But the views of the richest 10 percent are still highly predictive of public policy outcomes.

That's pretty disturbing, isn't it? I guess you could say we have the best government that money can buy.

Follow the Money

For the rich men thereof are full of violence, and the inhabitants thereof have spoken lies, and their tongue is deceitful in their mouth. — Micah 6:12

    The line comes from a movie, *All the President's Men*, adapted from the book of the same name penned by Carl Bernstein and Bob Woodward. The movie portrays how those two journalists exposed the Watergate scandal that ultimately brought about President Richard Nixon's political downfall. The scene is a dark parking garage where Woodward meets his informant, Deep Throat. When the reporter tries to coax information from his reluctant informant, he only receives a clue, "Follow the money."

    Sometimes it's obvious where the money went. Sometimes not. During the Iraq War over a billion dollars in cash went missing. To this day, its location remains unknown. But that's just pocket cash compared to a huge swindle perpetrated in plain view on the American people. On September 24, 2008, outgoing President George W. Bush announced that the economy was in serious danger. He said, "Easy credit—combined with the faulty assumption that home values would continue to rise—led to excesses and bad decisions. Many mortgage lenders approved loans for borrowers without carefully examining their ability to pay."

We Can Fix It

Several large financial institutions ran out of money, other banks "began holding on to their money, and lending dried up, and the gears of the American financial system began grinding to a halt." The president continued to explain the situation, then added,

> I'm a strong believer in free enterprise. So my natural instinct is to oppose government intervention. I believe companies that make bad decisions should be allowed to go out of business. Under normal circumstances, I would have followed this course. But these are not normal circumstances. The market is not functioning properly.

It wasn't. And most agree that without rescuing the banks the economy would have suffered even graver disruptions. The president continued, "Any rescue plan should also be designed to ensure that taxpayers are protected." However, few received protection, and not until well after the banks were on the mend. Continuing, he said, "It should make certain that failed executives do not receive a windfall from your tax dollars." In actuality, they used a fair bit of the bail-out funds to acquire other financial institutions, then patted themselves on their backs with bonuses. In order not to look too greedy, their bonuses were smaller than usual.

And what did the bill come to?

> Under our proposal, the federal government would put up to $700 billion taxpayer dollars on the line to purchase troubled assets that are clogging the financial system. In the short term, this will free up banks to resume the flow of credit to American families and businesses.

Follow the Money

As mentioned previously, because the banks weren't saddled with burdensome conditions on how to spend the money, they went on a spending spree instead of loaning their fresh funds as most expected they would. "And this will help our economy grow." It didn't. While the wealthy became more so, unemployment shot up and wages have stayed stagnant. Basically, the president, while pledging allegiance to an unregulated free market, did the sensible thing and pumped money into the financial system, in effect assuring members of that industry that others will pick up after them the next time they make a mess.

So how did that mess get started? Blame the invisible hand, the unregulated market. Hacker and Pierson claim it was Citigroup chairman Sanford Weill who was largely responsible for getting the Glass-Steagall Act repealed:

> When Citigroup formed in 1998, one of the top bankers involved joked at the celebratory press conference that any antitrust concerns could be dealt with easily: "Sandy will call up his friend, the President." Within a few months, the financial industry had mounted a successful campaign to repeal the Glass-Steagall Act which since the 1930s had prohibited powerful conglomerates of the sort Weill now headed on the grounds that they created conflicts of interest and impaired financial transparency.

The bundles of junk loans that traded freely prior to the 2008 financial crisis were so opaque one could have used them to view a solar eclipse. When borrowers couldn't pay down their mortgages, they learned the meaning of "too good to be true." The financial companies who bundled those bad loans had swindled

We Can Fix It

their investors. Mortgage brokers who sold those bad loans to property buyers told them that home prices would keep going up and that, by locking in the current price, they couldn't lose. They did lose, however, as home prices tumbled and their homes were no longer worth what they'd borrowed. Don't blame the real estate and mortgage brokers involved in the swindle. Most believed what they told their customers. Financial bubbles resemble those con men who play to people's greed by creating a sense of urgency—selling people deals that won't last long. If you meet someone trying to sell you a solid gold ring for $50.00 you can be sure it's really made of brass and not worth more than $10.00. But it's hard to turn down a deal that's too good to be true.

The reason we had a severe recession instead of a depression was because Washington acted quickly to stabilize the financial market. The banks were considered "too big to fail" so they were bailed out. Despite the president's desire to protect taxpayers, the majority of them received little relief. Once the banks were solvent again, the majority of American were left to fend for themselves, and even blamed by some for their imprudence.

The repealed Glass-Steagall Act was replaced with the Dodd-Frank Act. Writing on *Brookings.edu* in 2016, Ben Bernanke addresses progress toward preventing banks that were too big to fail (TBTF) from repeating their past mistakes. He said, "I see a lot of progress on the TBTF issue, more than the public appreciates. But more remains to be done to fully implement and calibrate the anti-TBTF program." Noting that other factors besides size needed consideration in order to prevent another financial crisis, he said:

"In particular, the government's strategy for ending TBTF addresses the deficiencies, noted above, of imposing arbitrary limits on bank size. Most obviously,

Follow the Money

the strategy does not make the mistake of treating size as the only determinant of systemic risk (e.g., capital surcharges depend on a variety of criteria). Particularly interesting, though, is that the government's strategy, by enlisting market forces and making good use of incentives, is more likely to lead to "right-sizing" of banks, where by "right-sizing" I mean getting right (from a social perspective) not only size (assets and liabilities) but also other dimensions of firm structure and organization that bear on systemic risk. My takeaway is not that the problem is solved—that will take more time—but rather that the current approach amounts to a process that will help us find the solution."

In June of 2017, however, Congress voted to dismantle many of the regulations imposed by Dodd-Frank according to Renae Merle writing on *Washingtonpost.com*. So far that hasn't happened because they've lacked sufficient Senate votes to turn their wish list into law.

Dismantling TBTF regulations heightens the possibility of another financial meltdown. It's reckless, but political opinions change like the wind under the right influences. During the recession begun in 2008, many politicians protested government stimulus spending because they felt it would weaken the dollar. In 2017, however, some of these same politicians voted to increase the national deficit by 1.4 trillion dollars over the next ten years. The tax act they passed was justified by the expectation that it would create jobs and stimulate the economy. This would be a great idea if the labor market wasn't already close to full employment and if the stock market wasn't already achieving historic highs. What the bottom 80 percent of Americans really need is higher wages and a less static economy. Income inequality fuels economic stagnation by reducing people's buying power. The 2017 tax act will increase inequality by lessening corporations' tax burden. This is

We Can Fix It

expected to boost workers wages, but will it? Early indicators are mixed. Some corporations have raised employee's wages. Others have paid large bonuses to their executives. Over time inequality will increase.

On December 14, 2017, John Cassidy, writing on *Newyorker.com* examined the recently released "World Inequality Report." He notes,

> The new report says that the surge in inequality, which has seen the share of over-all income and wealth of the country's top one per cent virtually double, is "largely due to massive educational inequalities, combined with a tax system that grew less progressive despite a surge in top labor compensation since the 1980s, and in top capital incomes in the 2000s."

He discusses how this tax act will add to income inequality. One way American workers will be burdened is that by 2027 every American except the wealthiest five percent will pay more in taxes. I wonder what makes those people so special? Cassidy concludes by quoting from an op-ed from a report author and his associates.

> In an op-ed timed to accompany the release of the World Inequality Report, Piketty and some of his colleagues warned that the G.O.P. tax bill will "turbocharge inequality in America" and make the country look "more and more like a rentier society." That sounds about right.

The new tax law won't reduce stagnant wages—increased inequality might make them worse. Current demand for low skill workers is about the same as their supply. In ten years when the tax cuts have expired many of these workers will have lost jobs to AI and

Follow the Money

robots. Currently there's an unfilled demand for technically-trained workers and that demand is expected to increase. Instead of creating a tax law that lines wealthy pockets, lawmakers should address economic stagnation by educating workers to do the jobs of the future. Perhaps lawmakers confuse a strong stock market with peoples' general welfare. The stock market is booming and the new tax law may help it boom more, but more than half of Americans own no stock at all.

    Americans were twice fooled in previous administrations with promises that tax cuts for the wealthy would trickle wealth down to them. Although money failed to trickle on both occasions, that didn't prevent lawmakers from trying voodoo economics for the third time. The Tax Cuts and Jobs Act of 2017 is designed to preserve and increase the worth of the wealthiest. The act passed and was signed into law despite a majority of Americans disapproving of it. Lawmakers hope that larger paychecks will change the the minds of these Americans.

    When banks face failure like they did in 2008, everyone hears about it. But some of the ways the wealthy game the system remain hidden. Reich describes how large corporations can, and do, avoid the consequences for bending the law to their advantage. They have a number of means at their disposal for influencing government. One way is to persuade friendly Congressmen to give them wrist slaps in lieu of steep fines. The public tends not to notice. What may seem a large number to an average person might be a pittance to a large corporation. When there's billions at stake, a million dollar fine is no great deterrent. Corporations can also persuade officials to overlook transgressions. "Another technique used by moneyed interests to squelch a law they dislike is to is to ensure Congress does not appropriate enough funds to enforce

We Can Fix It

it." But that's hardly their only trick, "An even quieter means of rescinding laws is to riddle them with so many loopholes and exceptions that they become almost impossible to enforce. Typically, such holes are drilled when agencies attempt, through rule making, to define what the laws mean or prohibit." In the case of Dodd-Frank, Wall Street's attempt to influence governance has resulted in endless delays of enforcement.

Since the rallying cry of the wealthy is less regulation, it's not uncommon for industry insiders to seek appointment to top positions in the very agencies that regulate their industries. Economists call this *regulatory capture* and it weakens and rolls back regulations while serving self-interests. Elites have no desire to modify regulations that further their interests. Charitable tax deductions are a powerful way to leverage wealth toward one's own interests. Reich says,

> (T)he 2005 analysis by Indiana University Center on philanthropy showed that even under the most generous assumptions only about a third of 'charitable' giving is targeted to helping poor people." Much of it goes to prep schools and private universities that primarily school the elite. This is money that could have financed public universities had it been taxed. Not only do the privileged benefit from attending elite schools, the government is essentially funding them by granting them tax deductions.

This may sound like a minor abuse of privilege, but it's a symptom of America's underlying classism. Joan C. Williams claims more urban and affluent Americans misunderstand the working class in her 2017 book, *White Working Class: Overcoming Class Cluelessness in America.*

Follow the Money

Americans assume college is a class escalator, and it can be for the nonelite kids who make it into Yale or Harvard. But few do. A recent study found that 38 colleges, including five in the Ivy League, have more students from the top 1% than from the entire bottom 60% of the income distribution.

She adds,

> The American higher education system operates as a "caste system: it takes Americans who grew up in different social strata and it widens the divisions between them," concludes public policy expert Suzanne Mettler.

Voters don't usually notice charitable donations that are subsidized by government, but these aren't the only invisible ways in which elites can leverage government for their own advantage. Rent-seeking occurs when scarcity adds to the amount that can be charged for a product or service. Scarcity, however, can be artificially created by groups seeking to create regulations which favor themselves. There are four ways in which special interests can gain unfair market advantages, Brink Lindsey and Steven Teles write in, *The Captured Economy: How the Powerful Enrich Themselves, Slow Down Growth, and Increase Inequality.*

Their examples of special interest rent-seeking come from finance, intellectual property, occupational licensing, and land use. Lack of competition, they argue, is one of the reasons behind income inequality. Enforcing antitrust laws would create more competition "But an absence of competition also comes from the affirmative use of government power, such as when incumbents are able to fend off challenges by constructing barriers to entry like licenses or intellectual property protection."

We Can Fix It

While no one wants to see a doctor lacking sufficient credentials, over-strenuous requirements can keep qualified physicians out of the game:

> Although graduation from a U.S. medical school is not required to obtain a medical license, completion of a U.S. residency program is ... The U.S. residency requirement, combined with highly restrictive policies on high-skill immigration, makes AMA power over medical school accreditation a powerful lever to constrict supply. Meanwhile, by historical accident the vast bulk of funding for residency slots is provided by Medicare, and for cost saving reasons the number of slots has been frozen since 1997. In 2016, for example, 8,640 graduates of accredited medical schools who applied for residencies—or roughly a quarter of all applicants—failed to be given a match.

If a quarter of new doctors can't find residencies, then shortages of doctors are bound to lead to higher healthcare costs. Should the AMA choose to loosen requirements enough to increase the supply of physicians, they would also be reducing the potential salaries of their members. Groups like the AMA lack incentives to increase membership and are likely to become even more restrictive in influencing licensing requirements. Unfortunately lawmakers receive most of their information from those most likely to engage in rent seeking. Such groups have both money and organization on their side while ordinary citizens lack both and are often unaware of potential rent seekers.

Silicon Valley is another source of rent seeking. Just recently one of Amazon's patents expired. This was for their one-click purchasing method. While there's nothing inherently inventive in a method that saves a

Follow the Money

mouse click, Amazon none-the-less gained an advantage over Barnes and Nobel with this dubious patent.

> It's easier now than in earlier years to obtain patents. "In 1982, the newly established Court of Appeals for the Federal Circuit (CAFC) was vested with exclusive appellate jurisdiction over patent cases. Since then, the CAFC has reshaped the law by lowering the standards for patentability and expanding the scope of patentable inventions to include software, business methods, and even parts of the human genome. As a result, the number of patents issued annually by the US Patent and Trademark Office has increased almost fivefold. ...

For this reason an entire industry buys patents in order to sue those who infringe upon them. The potential liability that one might be sued for accidentally using another company's patented method discourages innovators from developing new products. Loosely defined and over-enforced, patent laws are stifling start-ups, crushing competition, and preventing progress.

Tackling regulations that hide rent seeking won't be easy. Many of these are implemented on the state and local level. Others are implemented at the federal level. For these, Lindsey and Teles suggest a possible means to reduce regulatory rent seeking. Lobbyists provide much of the information used to create policies. Unfortunately, that information is often biased in favor of the organization providing it. Lindsey and Teles believe that legislators should use committees to acquire objective information:

> Congress needs to concentrate additional resources on top talent in committees, where staffers can fo-

cus on developing policy (rather than responding to constituents). The first-best option would be to reconstruct committee staff on the model of the Congressional Budget Office and the Government Accountability Office, which provide stable long-term employment to highly trained policy experts in a context of strict nonpartisanship.

This is a good approach, but other changes will also be needed if we are to create an economy that's more fair, more competitive, and more proactive in challenging the problems Americans face.

Cooperation or Chaos

Nothing truly valuable can be achieved except by the unselfish cooperation of many individuals. —Albert Einstein

Economic inequality has existed for thousands of years in a host of societies, claims historian Walter Scheidel. However, economic inequality could only get its start after humans began accumulating surpluses. And surpluses could only happen after societies transitioned from hunting and gathering to agriculture and herding. Along with surpluses, inherited wealth contributes to the widening of inequality. In societies in which economic inequality between the wealthy and the poor widened, "violent shocks" were the chief mechanism in re-equalizing wealth. These shocks, or "Four Horsemen of Leveling" are "mass mobilization warfare, transformative revolution, state failure, and lethal pandemics." The Four Horsemen of Leveling produce varied results in reducing income inequality. Sometimes these violent events achieve only small reductions in inequality, and sometimes they make it worse. Violence is by nature chaotic and unpredictable.

Two of the four horsemen have existed throughout history. These are state failure and lethal pandemics. The other two horsemen, mass mobilization warfare and transformative revolution, came into being during the twentieth century. Examples of these are the two

We Can Fix It

world wars, and the Communist revolutions in Russia and China. Up to 100 million died during equalization efforts in China and the Soviet Union. According to Scheidel, "... even though it would in principle have been possible for Lenin, Stalin, and Mao to achieve their goals with much more limited loss of life, sweeping expropriations crucially depended on the application of at least some violence and a credible threat of escalation."

While Scheidel argues that societies with extreme income inequality have often been leveled violently, he is unwilling to argue that the inequality has always caused violent leveling. While Scheidel treads cautiously, some economists argue more emphatically that extreme inequality will indeed result in social collapse. Reaffirming that people create markets and their rules, Reich warns of what can happen when elite groups mold those rules to serve their own interests,

> Over the last three decades, the rules have been shaped by large corporations, Wall Street, and very wealthy individuals in order to channel a large portion of the nation's total income and wealth to themselves. If they continue to have unbridled influence over the rules, and they gain control of the assets at the core of the new wave of innovations, they will end up with almost all the wealth, all the income, and all the political power. That result is no more in their interest than in the interests of the rest of the population, because under such conditions an economy and a society cannot survive.

Cooperation or Chaos

If Reich is correct, and current conditions continue, then violent leveling will occur. Should this happen, the next society will also become imbalanced in time and experience the same fate. Is this how humans always must live?

Research on great apes such as gorillas and chimpanzees shows that their social behavior is hierarchal, Scheidel notes. Therefore, it's reasonable to assume that human societies must be hierarchal as well. When Scheidel reviews studies of past and present hunting and gathering societies, however, he finds many to be more cooperative than hierarchal. In such societies, a bad day hunting or foraging could leave one hungry, but if one's neighbors share their food, one will survive. When cooperation has greater survival value than fending for oneself, that's what people will do. While hierarchy may exist in such societies, it cannot do so to a strong degree. Such societies would punish those who attempt to assume too much power. However, too much cooperation stifles competition 1and will limit a society's development. Cooperative societies may not be entirely non-hierarchal, but their hierarchies will be minimal and more fluid.

Once a society begins herding and farming, surpluses can accrue. And along with surpluses comes the hoarding of foodstuffs and other possessions, inheritance of property, and the creation of wealth. As wealth grows, so does inequality.

Inequality can be a good thing. It creates competition and competition inspires innovation. But growing inequality has its bad side:

> Thousands of years of history boil down to a simple truth: ever since the dawn of civilization, ongoing advances in economic capacity and state building favored growing inequality but did little if anything to bring it under control. Up to and including the

We Can Fix It

Great Compression of 1941 to 1950, we are hard pressed to identify reasonably well attested and nontrivial reductions in material inequality that were not associated, one way or another, with violent shocks.

The Great Compression as Scheidel uses it refers to the wartime and post-wartime period when labor was scarce and the wages of blue collar workers became closer to those of their college-educated white collar counterparts. The term can also be used in the broader sense of the more equal incomes that persisted through the 1970s. High progressive taxes kept incomes more equal through the Great Depression, World War II, and the Cold War. However, Scheidel doubts if such measures would be acceptable today.

I see few alternatives. Income disparity is extreme today as are the problems facing the world. Climate change will displace millions of the seven billion occupying the earth. Although robotics has the potential to improve our lives, that won't occur if the technology is hoarded by a wealthy elite. Additionally, economic benefits created by competition won't last when relatively few large corporations and wealthy elites own much of the wealth. The economy has been stagnant rather than thriving and it can't move forward as long as consumers have less and less purchasing power.

Scheidel discusses the possibility of non-violent leveling in his book's final section. Land reform is a process whereby wealthy land holders' land is redistributed to poor farmers. Land reform attempts have met with mixed results—sometimes resulting in more, not less, income inequality. In three instances, however, land reform resulted in lasting income leveling. The three countries involved were South Korea, South Vietnam, and Taiwan. In all three instances the United States urged those countries'

Cooperation or Chaos

leaders to implement land reform. The reason was the same for all three—land reform would help halt the spread of Communism. What's ironic is that land reform could never be attempted in the United States because the idea would be rejected as Communistic or socialistic in nature.

The Cold War fear of Communism was based on a potential reality, while labeling union organizers as socialists and Communists was more of a tactic by industrialists to keep wages low. While there are many affluent Americans who are socially aware and open minded, there are others who see their greatest good in preserving and growing their fortunes and defending their own class. For such people, Soviet Communists and union organizers are equally threatening.

Scheidel reminds us that human societies have taken a variety of shapes, from being highly cooperative to having extreme class segmentation. During the Cold War the United States feared that countries would fall to Communism, toppling one after another like dominoes. That's no longer likely. Yet the resistance remains. Universal Healthcare can't be implemented here because we reject anything vaguely socialist. Other well-developed countries more pragmatically protect their citizens from unaffordable healthcare crises. In the United States such ideas don't get off the ground because both citizens and politicians are bombarded with counter arguments. Useful dialog is stifled. Income inequality deprives many of prosperity, while the blare of wealthy interests deprive us from having our own voices heard.

Know Your Enemy

When a man's ways please the Lord, he maketh even his enemies to be at peace with him.—Proverbs 16:7

High gasoline prices during the 1980s made smaller Japanese vehicles more attractive than larger American ones. As a result, sales of domestic cars suffered as did unemployed American automotive workers in Detroit.

When a bar argument turned nasty, Vincent Chin was beaten so badly that he later died. Ironically, Chin was targeted as one of the Japanese who were taking American jobs. In fact, he was a working class American of Chinese ancestry. The two men who killed him were also working class Americans. Chin was tragically killed by men who assumed he was Japanese. He wasn't their enemy. If you want to face your enemy, you must first know who he is.

I've been talking about class warfare, but that isn't exactly accurate. A class is really a group of people associated with a certain degree of wealth, a certain set of beliefs, of customs, of preferences, etc. Individuals within a class can differ from one another on nearly all the traits by which they've been lumped together. Wealth itself may be the one factor that they share in common, yet what these people do with their wealth can vary widely. Of the eight wealthiest people in the world, one, Bill Gates, is a major philanthropist while another,

We Can Fix It

Warren Buffet, has said that it's wrong that he pays a lower tax rate than does his secretary. Class warfare is really about beliefs and activities which hurt the less fortunate. It's not about people.

This isn't really such a strange idea. We've been fighting a war on terror for some years now. It's a war not between countries, but between beliefs and activities—at least theoretically. The enemy is a real one, but he's hard to identify because he wears no uniform and hails from no particular country. To destroy such an enemy, he must first be understood. We have fought a War on Terror for years with only mixed results. It's likely that we haven't fully understood what motivates terrorists or addressed those social factors which breed terrorists.

Let's be clear. Many Americans are not financially secure. Recent tax changes will make their situations worse. The 2017 tax law contains continuing tax breaks for the wealthiest, expiring tax breaks for most Americans, and a huge debt burden placed upon all. The amount of property exempt from estate tax has doubled, helping the wealthy seed future ruling dynasties. As surely as self-interested wealthy voices have hijacked our democracy, worsening income inequality will hurt average Americans.

Just like with terrorism, our economic enemy is hard to identify. The enemy doesn't represent a class of people, only an ideology that some of its members share. But that ideology is a dangerous one that's harming our future.

Know Your Enemy

The enemy is crafty. He employs politicians who can be relied upon to offer poisons disguised as sweets. Sadly, there are those among us who continue to clamor after poisons, thinking them sweets. There are also those who when facing problems look for an enemy to blame. Our real enemy knows this and doesn't mind using a false enemy to evade scrutiny.

Most of us acknowledge that immigrants have richly contributed to our nation—we know that our railroads could not have been built without them. We also acknowledge that our own ancestors were immigrants. Yet many of us blame immigrants for taking our jobs. Some jobs may be taken by illegal immigrants, but many of us resist hard manual labor and favor better paying work. We're unwilling to be cheated by unscrupulous employers, risk dangerous and under compensated work injuries—or pay more for fast food and shoddy goods. However, it's not illegal immigrants who are the enemy. The true enemy is those who employ illegal immigrants to keep their costs down and profits up. By keeping their workers' wages low, they keep yours low as well. The enemy is not those who work. but those who hire them.

Writing for *Nytimes.com* on May 5, 2017, Neil Irwin ponders how close the U.S. economy is to full employment. He noted that wages were not rising even though the jobless rate was low. Given traditional assumptions about the relationship of demand to supply, wages should rise as unemployment decreases, but this hasn't happened. The article also notes that

We Can Fix It

Dallas construction companies and restaurants employing seasonal workers are struggling to fill jobs. These jobs are often performed by immigrants. However, Jens Manuel Krogstad, et al. writing on *pewresearch.org* in April 27, 2017, reports that between 2009 and 2016, the United States experienced a decrease of nearly a million unauthorized immigrants from Mexico. The claim that illegal immigrants take American jobs does not present a complete picture. Many of those lost jobs are low-paying and undesirable to most Americans. To be sure, many small business owners could not survive if forced to pay high wages. But I wonder if the desire by large corporations to reap unduly high profits isn't to a large degree responsible for keeping wages low.

If illegal immigrants may not be the enemies some think they are, what about members of certain ethnic or minority groups? In Hitler's Germany, Jews were the enemy. In the United States, enemies have fallen in and out of fashion. At various times, Irish and eastern Europeans have been popular enemies while some minorities, particularly Blacks, have been nearly perpetually popular enemies. In recent times, hate crimes directed at ethnic and minority groups have increased. The increase has often been associated with the increase in populism.

Populism, however, looks different today than it did in previous eras. Today many populists voice racist and xenophobic sentiments. They desire a return to old

Know Your Enemy

values and a nation that is once again largely white. Sitaraman tells of a more egalitarian time.

> ... in the early 1890s, there was a moment when biracial populism briefly emerged as a possibility. In Georgia, the agrarian radical Tom Watson campaigned on a platform of uniting poor blacks and whites. "You are kept apart that you may be separately fleeced of your earnings," Watson declared. "You are made to hate each other because upon that hatred is rested the keystone of the arch of financial despotism which enslaves you both. You are deceived and blinded that you may not see how this race antagonism perpetuates the monetary system which beggars both."

Watson's movement was ultimately defeated but his point is well taken. Immigrants who pick lettuce take jobs that few others desire. Yet many of the new populists want to send them back where they came from, claiming that they're taking their jobs. Those who would control us encourage this type of thinking. It distracts people from the real issues. An agenda that primarily serves the highly wealthy pushes the economy in the wrong direction. Those who are poor become more so, while those in the middle are edged closer to poverty.

Former *New York Times* reporter Chris Hedges came from a working class family and received a scholarship to attend an elite prep school.

> Going back and forth between that world of an elite prep school and this mill town in Maine—Mechanic Falls—I realized that in terms of native intelligence and aptitude, there were people in my family who were as gifted as anyone in my prep school. The

difference was that they, like most of the working poor, were never given a chance.

Though he met many sons of wealthy families, Hedges remained an outsider due to class. He has this to say about his schoolmates:

> The rich have disdain for anyone who does not belong to their inner circle. They believe that their wealth and privilege is conferred upon them because of their superior attributes. They define themselves not by what they are in private—in private they are usually bastards—but by the public persona created for them by publicity. They see their possessions and power, which in most cases they inherited, as natural and proper because they believe they are inherently better than others. Balzac said that behind every great fortune lies a great crime. He got that right.
>
> All these families—the Mellons, the Rockefellers, the Carnegies, the Morgans—started out as gangsters. They hired gun thugs to murder union organizers and strikers. We had the bloodiest labor wars in the industrialized world. Hundreds of workers were killed. ...
>
> The refinement of the rich is a veneer. They can afford good manners because they use others—including the machinery of state—to carry out their dirty work. They often know the names of the great authors and artists, but they are culturally and intellectually bankrupt. They are consumed by gossip, a pathological yearning for status and obsessed by brands and possessions ... They talk mostly

Know Your Enemy

about money—the money they made, the money they are making and the money they will make. They are Philistines.

    Using money to chase after more money when one already has more than a lifetime's supply is not a legitimate lifestyle. To be legitimate, one's lifestyle requires aspirations, values, obstacles and efforts to overcome them. A money-driven life resembles the life of a hamster ceaselessly running on an exercise wheel—keeping busy without actually going anywhere. This is madness. Two things can fuel greed—having too little—and having too much. A society that has a broad middle class, with few people at extreme ends of either poverty or over-abundance, is inherently a more healthy one.
    The middle class has narrowed and those struggling to stretch their paychecks from one to the next have increased. Yet not all Americans feel as Hedges does about the wealthy. Joan C. Williams quotes Eric Sansoni who moved from the working class into the professional class, "There's an almost mystical desire among the working class to see a rich person from the upper class reach out to them." This echos the theme Horatio Alger Jr. made popular in his rags-to-riches books. While writers throughout history have condemned the wealthy, fairy tales are jammed with wealthy royals, and with commoners like Cinderella who attract their notice. Humans are hierarchal beings—we seek status and admire those who have it. If you've been bankrupt on several occasions and litigated against several hundred times, you might still become a leader if you're also wealthy and a television star. We have a tendency to overlook the faults of those whose traits we admire. There's a belief among the working class, Williams notes, that the wealthy became so by pulling themselves up by their bootstraps through hard work and cleverness. And some did. Many others

We Can Fix It

inherited their wealth, however, and are no more clever or hardworking than anyone else.

It's easy to believe whatever we do about the wealthy because they are beyond our inspection. They don't eat where we eat or live where we live. In olden days when the king rode by, we bowed our heads and never caught a glimpse of his Majesty. Nor do we see the new aristocrats as they fly above us in their private jets.

If we make heroes of the wealthy, we resent professionals, at least if we're not professionals ourselves, Williams tells us:

> Daily life reinforces admiration of the rich but resentment of professionals. Most working-class people have little contact with the truly rich ... but they suffer class affronts from professionals every day: the doctor who unthinkingly patronizes the medical technician, the harried office worker who treats the security guard as invisible, the overbooked business traveler who snaps at the TSA agent. Remember: class isn't just about money. Everything we do is class-marked.

In the middle of the last century, working Americans enjoyed increasingly better lifestyles and confidence that their careers were stable and promotions were a possibility. Today they face numerous uncertainties. In October of 2017, Joe Neel on *Npr.org* reported on a poll in which Americans from different groups were asked about their experience of discrimination. Whites make up the majority of Americans and a smaller percentage of this group claimed to experience discrimination. None-the-less, a surprising 55 percent of whites felt themselves to be victims of discrimination. In fact, in every group polled a majority felt themselves to be victims of discrimination. This suggests to me that

Know Your Enemy

Americans no longer feel unified. Tom Watson was right. Division distracts us from seeing our real enemy clearly.

Weapons of Mass Deception

Doublethink means the power of holding two contradictory beliefs in one's mind simultaneously, and accepting both of them.
—George Orwell

The receptivity of the masses is very limited, their intelligence is small, but their power of forgetting is enormous. In consequence of these facts, all effective propaganda must be limited to a very few points and must harp on these in slogans until the last member of the public understands what you want him to understand by your slogan. —Adolf Hitler

Now that the enemy is known, we must know ourselves. We must understand our own weaknesses and strengths to prevent our enemy from undermining our strengths and taking advantage of our weaknesses. We do ourselves more harm than our enemy ever could by not cultivating self-understanding.

The American Dream leads us to believe that our hard effort will bring us career advancement. But for most, upward mobility is no longer possible. In many rural communities and former manufacturing hubs, the good jobs have left, and the remaining jobs don't pay well. Many lost their property during the 2008 recession and now struggle to regain lost years of progress. That same recession and its slow-growth recovery also detoured millennials hoping to establish career paths. But even before the recession began, opportunities for upward mobility were fewer than during earlier times. Movement from the lower-middle to the upper-middle class has become more difficult, yet far easier than movement from a lower class to the lower-middle class. The lower one's income is, the lower is one's chance of moving upward. The reality for many is economic uncertainty. Many live from paycheck to paycheck with no savings to fall back on. If the American Dream is sliding away, what dreams are left?

Plenty apparently. Kurt Anderson reports in the *Atlantic* in September 2017 that people are indulging in magical thinking. The trend began during the 1960s with its emphasis on self understanding and expression. It morphed into a belief that so-called conventional reality was not to be trusted because elites controlled the information we received. Because conventional truth had been hijacked, only personal truth had value. Today personal truth seems to have triumphed. In January 2017, the president was asked if it wasn't perilous to make an unsupported claim. He replied, "Not at all—because many people feel the same way that I do."

This hits at the heart of the problem. People are choosing their beliefs based on how they feel about issues rather than on reason and facts. Anderson calls it Fantasyland, a personal reality that draws on conspiracy theories, distorted web memes, and entertainment masquerading as factual information.

Weapons of Mass Deception

These people have lost the ability to discern what's real from what's make believe.

Anderson details the changes in popular academic thought since the 1960s to explain how people currently form their beliefs. While Anderson's theory is useful, popular academic trends can only impact social behavior to a limited degree. Fantasyland has infiltrated all walks of life and can't simply be blamed on a popular, yet naive, view of relativism. People have always enjoyed stories and always known the difference between fiction and real life. But something has changed. There may always have been people living aspects of their lives in Fantasyland, but it's easier to live there now due to the Internet and increased social stratification. During Williams' youth, Americans were less class conscious.

> Although my family was wealthy, my mom shopped at Sears and the A&P, I went to public school, and everyone watched the evening news with Walter Cronkite. Today, the professional elite sends their kids to private schools, shops at Whole Foods, and reads Slate instead of watching Fox.

We increasingly isolate ourselves among those of our own class and those sharing our beliefs. A belief system that serves as a protective cocoon will shield one from complexity and doubt, but it will also obstruct one's wider view.

The ancient Greeks are credited with pioneering democracy. They employed a tool called logic, but it wasn't a perfect tool. Some, like Socrates, used logic to seek truth. Others, the Sophists, taught logic as a persuasion tool of use to future politicians. Writing in *Scientific American* in February 2018, Matthew Fisher, et al. discuss two types of argument: *arguing to learn* and *arguing to win*. The aim of the first is agreement while that of the second is victory. Socrates argued to learn while his better paid rivals, the Sophists, argued to win.

Some writers, including Fisher et al., believe that Americans live in a "time of rising tribalism." I think of tribal behavior as exhibiting a sense of loyalty like being a Cub fan who can't imagine ever switching his allegiance to another team. If I lived in an earlier time I wouldn't dream of leaving my tribe to join another tribe. Tribalism works great for small societies and for sport fans. Under tribalism your team is always right even when it's wrong. Tribalism won't work in a democracy of millions.

Arguing to learn allows viewpoints to interact and evolve into consensus, or in compromise. This is what America's founders had in mind. Initially there were no political parties in America. At other times parties held bipartisan dialog. Not today.

The ancient Greeks understood the difference between the two types of argument and some held that arguing to win was a corrupt practice. That didn't stop wealthy Greek citizens from sending their children to Sophist teachers to learn persuasion techniques.

Past research shows that people tend to be either objectivists or relativists regarding moral and political issues. Objectivists believe issues only have one correct solution, while relativists are more likely to argue "it depends." When asked to sit near someone with opposing views, objectivists position themselves at a greater distance than do relativists. With this research in mind, Fisher et al. suspected that argumentation style could affect one's mindset. They first asked experimental subjects about their views on a variety of

Weapons of Mass Deception

issues. Then they matched each subject with another who held opposing views and asked them to connect online. Half were asked to seek information. The other half were urged to win. When the subjects finished their 15-minute online tasks, they were asked if the subject they had argued had an objectively true answer. Subjects who argued to win were more likely to believe in objectively true answers than were those who argued to learn. Additionally, some objectivist subjects shifted their views during the experiment.

Experiments like this have limitations. An experiment may shift views temporarily, but it is foolish to assume such shifts will be permanent. We also tend to develop habits. I believe arguing to win can become a habit, and not a good one. Arguing to win does not generate productive solutions to social problems.

We are not entirely the rational beings that we think we are. Emotions play a strong part in our beliefs and their maintenance. Propaganda peddlers know this and do their best to convince us through our emotions. We make it easier for them when we seek out media that works us into an emotional froth or hypnotizes us by endlessly repeating the same points—often in the absence of evidence.

In *1984*, George Orwell describes the audience of the Two Minutes Hate, a propaganda pep rally. As they stood watching a giant screen,

> A hideous ecstasy of fear and vindictiveness ... seemed to flow through the whole group of people like an electric current, turning one even against one's will into a grimacing, screaming lunatic. And yet the rage that one felt was an abstract, undirected emotion which could be switched from one object to another like the flame of a blowlamp.

We Can Fix It

We have no Two Minutes Hate here. Instead, we listen to talk radio rhetoric for far longer than two minutes while commuting to work. Our host is emotionally persuasive and repetitive. If the radio host is successful, we'll arrive at work feeling confidence in those who are right and anger toward those who are wrong. If instead, we tune in to an interview, discussion, or debate, we'll arrive at work with more questions than certainties. From questions, new answers may come. And from answers, social progress arises. [See note at the end of this chapter]

If we're to take charge of our own political destinies we have to make an effort to cut through superficial issues and understand those that are substantial. This means seeking out multiple news sources, listening to multiple opinions, and being willing to stretch our beliefs past their boundaries. Social Media is particularly dangerous. Every "like" on social media is a vote that says, "This is who I am. Show me something else I like." It doesn't take very long before the media service has a very clear picture of you. Great customer service, huh? Only it's not. Micah L. Sifry, writing in The Nation, on October 30, 2017, states, "You are not Facebook's customer; you are its product. Facebook's only true constituency is its millions of advertisers." Social Media wants your profile for its advertisers, not because it cares for your welfare.

Our nation's founders were thoughtful men who read, pondered, and debated. Today we don't take time to think deeply because we're constantly plugged into media—radio, television or the Internet. The media moves and we react, emotionally and without taking time to ponder what we take in. And what we allow in has more influence over us than we realize.

We think of ourselves as conscious actors becoming aware and acting upon our awareness. Yet, our awareness, what we call consciousness, is only a small part of what goes on in our brains. Consciousness is like an iceberg's tip—visible above the water's surface. Much of what runs us is below the surface and well beneath our awareness. Most of us realize this to some extent. After all, our hearts pump and our lungs breathe without our awareness most of the time. But most of us don't realize the extent to which non-conscious mental activity controls our behavior.

In his book, *Incognito: The Secret Lives of the Brain*, David Eagleman tells us that the brain is composed of interacting systems, or modules, running a myriad of mental routines, and very little of this activity makes it into our awareness. It's as if our brains are run by a team of rivals with different viewpoints to match different circumstances. When teammates interact appropriately, we make good decisions most of the time.

Psychologists find that most of us carry hidden biases. At our deepest levels are distrustful guardians, rivals harboring thoughts that we'd never verbalize. But substances like alcohol, or strong emotions, can disturb the balance between the rivals in our brains. After visiting a Jewish friend, actor Mel Gibson, was arrested for driving under the influence of alcohol. Later, a sober Gibson apologized for the anti-Semitic remarks he made while intoxicated. The question arises, who is the real Mel Gibson, the sober friend of a Jew or the drunken anti-Semite? Eagleman's answer is that both are real, because Gibson's brain, like everyone's, is composed of interacting rivals. Most of us behave in socially appropriate ways most of the time. But, there are times when our emotions can show us sides of ourselves we'd rather not acknowledge. For the most part, however, we go along unaware of many passing emotions, yet led, to some degree, by them. Media is constantly barraging our senses and emotions with information—if we don't compensate by taking time to

We Can Fix It

mull things over, bias and distortion can creep into our views. We may not be aware of our biases, but politicians and advertisers can find them. And they know how to appeal to them. If we don't seek out and engage other people with other views—if we allow ourselves to be barraged with repetitive and emotionally arousing messages—we live in a distorted world, a Fantasyland.

The viewpoint of those who join cults or elite military units resembles the viewpoint of those with tunnel vision, according to Shankar Vedantam's *The Hidden Brain: How our Unconscious Minds Elect Presidents, Control Markets, and Save our Lives*. Those with tunnel vision narrow their mental focus, attending to the views and aims of their particular group, and not to those of the world at large.

A few hours before more than 900 People's Temple members died after drinking poisoned Kool-Aid in Jonestown, five other people were killed at Guyana's Port Katuna Airstrip. Larry Layton, another People's Temple member, had gunned them down. Larry had volunteered for a suicide mission to bring down a plane returning to the United States. The mission went awry—Larry survived, but five of the plane's passengers did not. Why had Larry Layton volunteered? He was living in a tunnel: "As he sat in his prison cell in Guyana, it slowly became apparent to Layton that the world he had inhabited for so long was not the real world, that it was only a tunnel that had appeared to be the whole world."

Today the phrase, "drink the Kool-Aid," refers to an uncritical acceptance of what another person or group tells you. You don't have to be a cult member to "drink the Kool-Aid"—merely an uncritical thinker, influenced by the "hidden brain" rather than its more rational side.

The "hidden brain" is useful because it helps us make decisions quickly. However, those decisions are not always correct. Knowing when to run is useful in a dangerous environment but most contemporary decisions require more reflection than flight. Media encourages our natural inclination to maintain our belief systems, to seek confirming and emotionally pleasing information. It becomes easy to begin living in a tunnel and not see the wider world. Reporting an experiment in Scientific American, in April 2017, Walter Quattrociocchi notes,

> When we reconstructed the social networks of our two groups (science news readers and fans of conspiracy theories), we discovered a surprising statistical regularity: as the number of likes for a specific type of narrative increased, the probability of having a virtual social network composed solely of users with the same profile also increased. In other words, the more you are exposed to a certain type of narrative, the greater the probability that all your Facebook friends will have the same news preferences. The division of social networks into homogeneous groups is crucial to understanding the viral nature of the phenomena. These groups tend to exclude anything that does not fit with their worldview.

Those who understand the workings of social groups can tailor messages to them. The Russians did just that in the 2016 U.S. election. The Russians, of course, aren't the only ones who are eager to know what Fantasylands people live in. On November 14, 2017, the Brookings Institute shared remarks made three days earlier by Tom Wheeler on its website, *Brookings.edu*.

> For a century-and-a-half, the economic model for media companies was to assemble information in

We Can Fix It

order to attract eyeballs for advertising. To maximize that reach, traditional outlets curated that information for veracity and balance. In stark contrast, the curation of social media platforms is not for veracity, but for advertising velocity.

Truthfulness is irrelevant to belief manipulation. Understanding and maintaining tunnels is more useful to manipulators.

In early 2017, historian Timothy Snyder released his book, *On Tyranny: Twenty Lessons from the Twentieth Century*. Snyder summarizes Victor Klemperer's observations on how truth dies. In the first phase authority openly lies. In the second, slogans are endlessly repeated. In the final phase, magical thinking is adopted. Once truth is dead, marketers can flood our tunnels with the messages they want us to hear. But we haven't yet reached the point where our government is tyrannical, or have we? Snyder reminds us:

> We certainly face, as did the ancient Greeks, the problem of oligarchy—ever more threatening as globalization increases differences in wealth. The odd American idea that giving money to political campaigns is free speech means that the very rich have far more speech, and so in effect far more voting power, than other citizens. We believe that we have checks and balances, but have rarely faced a situation like the present: when the less popular of the two parties controls every lever of power at the federal level, as well as the majority of statehouses. The party that exercises such control proposes few policies that are popular with the society at large, and several that are generally unpopular—and thus must either fear democracy or weaken it.

Weapons of Mass Deception

It's easy to isolate oneself in a tunnel. It happens by accident and through habit. Those who manipulate us hope we never leave our tunnels. However, we owe it to ourselves and our society to emerge from our tunnels into the open, to see clearly and act upon reality.

Human brains can achieve marvels, yet they also have their short-comings. In addition to our "hidden brain" we have hidden biases. Extensive lists can be found online, but I want to concentrate on two of our brain biases. The first is called *confirmation bias*. It describes our tendency to seek arguments and information that confirm what we already believe. The second bias, *belief perseverance*, describes a tendency to defend what we believe when encountering contradictory information. We most readily find reasons to bolster our beliefs when they closely impact our self-concept and worldvision.

Overcoming belief perseverance can be difficult. Writing on *Scientificamerican.com* in 2012, Carrie Arnold states,

> Correcting misinformation, however, isn't as simple as presenting people with true facts. When someone reads views from the other side, they will create counterarguments that support their initial viewpoint, bolstering their belief of the misinformation.

Vigorously presenting facts to someone resisting belief-change strengthens their misbeliefs. Rather than draw attention to debunked myths, "Another way to combat misinformation is to create a compelling narrative that incorporates the correct information, and focuses on the facts rather than dispelling myths—a technique called 'de-biasing.'" Being confrontational is unproductive. Instead, look for areas of agreement and build your counter narrative on those.

We Can Fix It

If it's disheartening to discuss our hidden brain and its hidden biases, consider the astounding feats of discovery that the brain sometimes performs. Einstein used his slack time at the Swiss patent office to ponder the nature of gravity. From this came the theory of relativity. Postmortem analysis of Einstein's brain revealed nothing special about it. Yet his "ordinary" brain revealed our ideas of space and time to be illusions. Over one hundred years later science has confirmed Einstein's ideas and employed them in advanced technology, yet we still live our lives as if space and time were not the illusions science tells us they are.

Robert Wright compares the findings of modern psychology to concepts in Buddhism in his 2017 book, Why Buddhism Is True. Wright echoes Buddhist thought by identifying emotion as a chief cause of delusion in our lives.

> It's in the nature of feelings to make it hard to tell the valuable ones from the harmful ones, the reliable from the misleading. One thing all feelings have in common is that they were originally 'designed' to convince you to follow them. They feel right and true almost by definition. They actively discourage you from viewing them objectively.

Wright reconfirms the idea that our brain is made of competing rivals (systems, modules).

> Buddhist thought and modern psychology converge on this point: in human life as it's ordinarily lived, there is no one self, no conscious CEO, that runs the show; rather, there seem to be a series of selves that take turns running the show—and, in a sense, seizing control of the show. If the way they

Weapons of Mass Deception

seize control of the show is through feelings, it stands to reason that one way to change the show is to change the role feelings play in everyday life. I'm not aware of a better way to do that than mindfulness meditation.

Wright reminds us that several centuries ago, "David Hume wrote that human reason is 'the slave of the passions.'" In other words, reason doesn't kick in until emotions get it working.

> The more we learn about the functioning of the brain, the more sense Hume's view makes. Joshua Greene, a neuroscientist at Harvard, has written of a particular region in the prefrontal cortex called the dorsolateral prefrontal cortex: The DLPFC, the seed of abstract reasoning, is deeply interconnected with the dopamine system, which is responsible for placing values on objects and actions. From the neural and evolutionary perspective, our reasoning systems are not independent logic machines. They are outgrowths of more primitive mammalian systems for selecting rewarding behaviors ...

One goal of meditation is to become more aware of oneself in the world. By increasing awareness, one can reduce the degree of delusion that one experiences. A meditator typically concentrates on the inflow and outflow of his breath or upon the repetition of a mantra. As he does so, thoughts will arise. The idea is to gently let them go and to return to your concentration. Psychology has a name for the thoughts that arise when you're thinking nothing in particular. These random thoughts arise in the "default mode network" (DMN).

The DMN is what your mind is using when it's wandering.

We Can Fix It

As for where the mind wanders to: well, lots of places, obviously, but studies have shown that these places are usually in the past or the future; you may ponder recent events or distant, strong memories; you may dread upcoming events or eagerly anticipate them; you may strategize about how to head off some looming crisis or fantasize about romancing the attractive person in the cubicle next to yours. What you're generally *not* doing when your mind is wandering is directly experiencing the present moment.

Meditation offers a way of "experiencing the present moment" by stilling the default mode network. Meditation increases activity in brain areas associated with executive function and reasoning according to Katherine Martucci, et al. writing on *Wakehealth.edu,* It also reduces activity in areas associated with emotions.

Although Robert Wright mentions that other activities have benefits similar to meditation, he doesn't discuss them. Any activity requiring concentration will reduce activity in the DMN. However, meditation is also deeply relaxing and helps one observe ones' stray thoughts non-judgmentally. I believe that other contemplative activities such as walking, fishing, painting, praying, etc. can have effects similar to meditation. Regardless, such relaxing activities can help reduce anxiety. The circus is loud and non-stop. It manipulates us emotionally like we were puppets on strings. Walk away from all that emotionality. Turn off your radio next time you drive to work.

Getting democracy working again will require calm and civility. Meditate, or do something similar. Additionally, be on guard for falsehoods. Make an effort to check the sources of any news you read or hear. Here's why it matters: Amy Mitchell, et al. discussed a

Weapons of Mass Deception

study of online news readers on Pew Research's *Journalism.org*. The study found that online news readers are about equally likely to choose social media or news organizations to find news. However, those who favored social media for their news were least likely to remember the source of the story. News presented on social media often features sensational headlines which don't hold up under closer inspection. Often the headlines are only negligibly supported by the original news story. Unfortunately, readers don't always click through to the underlying story. Make it a point to be dubious and read further. Snyder reminds us, "If we are serious about seeking the facts, we can each make a small revolution in the way the Internet works. If you are verifying information for yourself, you will not send on fake news to others."

    Another step you can take to be a well-informed citizen is to brush up on, and make use of, the rules of logic. Social media burns with argumentative strangers insulting one another. One eternal cheap-shot, non-argument is called the Ad Hominem argument. It works by discrediting a person rather than by attacking his argument. Unfortunately the Internet is rife with such name-calling and it's easy to fire back with names of one's own. That does no good; it only creates anger and fuels tribalism. No one has ever been convinced of anything through disrespect. If we're going to repair our democracy and our environment, we've got to be unified. Approach people as potential allies by listening respectfully to what they have to say and then building on what you already agree on.

    The title tells it all: *Not a scientist: how politicians mistake, misrepresent, and utterly mangle science.* Dave Levitan's 2017 book describes the various ways politicians distort science. They oversimplify, cherry-pick, ridicule, and invent science in their speeches. One technique touches upon the subject before redirecting

We Can Fix It

discussion to an objection as then Speaker of the House, John Boehner, did in 2014, "'Listen, I'm not qualified to debate the science over climate change.' He followed up by saying that any efforts to deal with the problem would wreck the economy—which most experts also agree is totally untrue." The economy as a whole would improve if climate change were strongly addressed. However, mitigation could damage business for climate change deniers—unless they reinvent themselves by diversifying and expanding how they do business. In an unregulated free market, a business model that survived through special favors and a clinging to an obsolete technology would fail as it should. Competition should drive a strong economy, but when too much wealth clings to the top, competition is discouraged.

Levitan reminds us to speak up when we hear science being abused:

> Vigilance is the only antidote against a flood of misinformation, deception, and backwardness. If you spot any particularly egregious misuses of science from the President or any other politicians, call your Senator or House representative—let them know that you want Washington to curtail its anti-science ways.

[Note: For decades television and radio broadcasters adhered to the Fairness Doctrine, which urged them to provide access to those who held opposing opinions. Originally, the Fairness Doctrine made sense because broadcasters were so few it was feared their opinions would bias their audiences. As cable television became popular, the vast increase in viewable broadcasters made it seem that the Fairness Doctrine was no longer required. Further, it was seen as an infringement of free speech.

Weapons of Mass Deception

The Fairness Doctrine was repealed during the Reagan era. During a subsequent era, President Clinton signed the 1996 Telecommunications Act into law. Deregulation did not bring competition as was promised. Instead, media ownership fell into fewer hands. Additionally, without a Fairness Doctrine to restrain them, news broadcasters could now substitute emotionally charged opinion for news that was objective but bland.

Fake news was not invented by the Russians. It's been with us since the Clinton era. That said, I'm reluctant to accuse anyone of purveying fake news. Additionally, there's a word I'm reluctant to use. That word is "brainwashing."

None-the-less, I should mention the 2015 motion picture and 2016 DVD, *The Brainwashing of My Dad*. In her documentary, Jen Senko describes how her father's radio listening habits changed as he began driving a new route to work. Over time, his views changed as well. Senko's father grew angrier and less tolerant. Years later, family members intervened by selecting radio and television content for him. The father's views changed once again. His intolerance and anger melted away.

There's a saying, "You are what you eat." A junk food diet will build an unhealthy body. A diet of junk news will build an unhealthy mind. Fortunately the effects of both junk food and junk news can be reversed through a change of diet.]

Getting Even

Strange is our situation here upon earth. Each of us comes for a short visit, not knowing why, yet sometimes seeming to a divine purpose. From the standpoint of daily life, however, there is one thing we do know: That we are here for the sake of other men—above all for those upon whose smile and well-being our own happiness depends, for the countless unknown souls with whose fate we are connected by a bond of sympathy. —Albert Einstein

The United States doesn't have a formal aristocracy. The ninth section of the first article of its constitution prohibits our government from bestowing titles. That section says, "No Title of Nobility shall be granted by the United States: And no Person holding any Office of Profit or Trust under them, shall, without the Consent of the Congress, accept of any present, Emolument, Office, or Title, of any kind whatever, from any King, Prince, or foreign State." The founders made it very clear that they wanted a classless democracy.

Instead of a formal aristocracy, what we now have is a wealthy elite—some call it an oligarchy—who have largely hijacked the national agenda. This is even worse for our people than an aristocracy would have been. The French phrase, *noblesse oblige,* describes an unwritten guideline European nobles were expected to follow. It implies that the ruling class has an obligation to guard the welfare of the less fortunate. There is no such implicit obligation in a philosophy that believes in acquiring and preserving money at the expense of everyone else's welfare. Unlike the Robber Barons whose ruthlessness built railroads, those who currently strive after money lack guiding principles. Their philosophy is without social value. Endlessly chasing money, they are like a dog endlessly chasing its own tail. The dog is merely amusing itself, but the elite are destroying our society.

Consider what happened to Europe's royalty. In order to maintain international harmony, cousins from different countries married one another. In so doing, their genes became inbred. That is why so many from the royal houses were hemophiliacs. With only 0.01 percent of this nation gaining an ever increasing portion of its wealth, and with those people isolating themselves from the less affluent, that's bound to happen here unless they destroy the country first. Becoming genetically inbred will take time, but many of these people are already *conceptually* inbred. Without a diversity of ideas and opinions reaching them, they reflect only those ideas and opinions shared by their class and not on others which could improve the nation as a whole.

They have nothing useful to say and they're saying it too loudly. We needn't silence them, but we must have our voices heard as well. In *Citizens United v. FEC*, the Supreme Court decided that corporate persons had the right to spend what they pleased in exercising their free speech. The problem here is that corporate persons are

Getting Even

not the same as flesh-and-blood persons. Corporations do not die as people do. They cannot take the fifth amendment in their self defense. And they are not taxed as people are. None-the-less, the Supreme Court gave them the same free speech rights as other citizens. In so doing, the Court favored one class of persons over another. Although everyone is free to spend as much as they want to have their voices heard, only wealthy and corporate persons have enough cash to do so. The relatively egalitarian society that Jefferson and others envisioned for this country is not written anywhere in the Constitution, but it's hinted at in its first article. Most Americans assume we live in a democracy, or at least we should. But when individual American voices are silenced in the roar of money-powered ones, and when the popular will is ignored, then our democracy is endangered. At the very least, we need laws limiting how much corporations can spend to influence elections. The amount should be no higher than what an average American can afford to spend. If corporations were limited to spending no more than—say $5,000.00 per election—there would be a lot less misleading information filling mailboxes, and a lot more trees spared the axe.

The issue of corporate personhood must also be addressed. Corporations are inherently privileged with immortality if properly managed. Without poor health and death to slow them down, corporations can continue to accumulate wealth and political influence. Given so great an advantage, corporations deprive individuals of the opportunities they once had to farm their own land and work in their own trades. While there's no returning to yesterday's economy, new opportunities could arise if extreme inequality didn't interfere. We'll need first to destroy the artificial aristocracy that corporate privilege creates and bestows on corporations and their owners. If a more equal playing field is to be restored, language defining the rights of corporate persons, as distinguished from human persons, must be written into law.

The conditions that favored a more egalitarian society during the founders' time no longer exist. It's no longer possible to move west to homestead a farm. However, the wider, more prosperous middle class that grew and thrived in the middle twentieth century is a goal still within reach. To achieve it, we must return to the high graduated taxes of the post-Depression years. Doing so need not hurt corporations, but their greed-driven model must change. Corporations thrived under a stakeholder model that considered the public, the employees, as well as the shareholders. With higher progressive taxes, executives are less tempted to squeeze out high salaries for themselves and their cronies. Instead, they'll put more of their energy into serving the public. Less to show after taxes also encourages reinvesting money into research and development.

Currently we treat corporations as privileged persons. Corporations are taxed at a flat rate while people are taxed at graduated rates. We must make it

Getting Even

clear that corporations don't have the same rights as humans and there's no reason to grant them special privileges. We could do a good deal of equalizing by taxing corporations on a steeply graduated progressive basis, while also considering the ratio of employees to company size and the income differential between the wages of the highest- and lowest-paid employees. Companies with more egalitarian pay scales would be taxed at a lower rate than those that paid out obscene salaries to their CEOs.

In addition to corporations, the wealthy elite have themselves become an artificial aristocracy. Jefferson counted the repeal of the entail, or the hereditary right of primogeniture, as one of his proudest achievements. Adam Smith would have agreed. He said,

> A power to dispose of estates for ever is manifestly absurd. The earth and the fullness of it belongs to every generation, and the preceding one can have no right to bind it up from posterity. Such extension of property is quite unnatural.

Theodore Roosevelt firmly favored high progressive taxes on inherited wealth. The estate tax has been part of our tax code since 1916, claims Thomas M. Shapiro in his book. *Toxic inequality: how America's wealth gap destroys mobility, deepens the racial divide, & threatens our future*. Continuing to address the estate tax, Shapiro adds:

> In its present form, it is the clearest symbol of the power of today's superwealthy families to pass along unearned privileges. Very few estates, just 18

in every 10,000, pay any estate taxes. The 2015 exclusion level below which wealth is protected is nine times higher than it was in 1997, and the top tax rate is 37.5 percent lower. In a better world, we would capture far more revenue from the transfer of unearned property and wealth from one generation to the next in order to provide real opportunities for those not born into affluence and who will inherit little money, or none.

The 2017 tax law nearly doubled the amount exempt from estate taxes. Although they'll revert to their 2017 tax exempt amount in a few years, that amount was already too high to effectively forestall increasing inequality. Not only is a strong estate tax needed to restore the American Dream, so too is a strong progressive tax. Money should be raised and put to use paying down our national debt, developing renewable energy, and planning for a changing environment due to climate change.

We can't simply continue operating an economy that serves greedy appetites rather than human necessities. Greed makes people stingy and close-minded while healthy competition and cooperation can create a future that serves humanity. In order to have an economy in which the majority thrive, we've got to bring inequality down by balancing out the enormous amounts of privately-held wealth with spending in the public interest. The government should actively fund groups and individuals with socially useful ideas. We should create a society in which labor is rewarded, initiative is acknowledged, and the public good is served. But the government will require funds to accomplish this and corporations and the wealthy will need to do their part in providing it. This does not mean that everyone's taxes need to go up, but the 20 percent of the

Getting Even

population that holds 90 percent of American wealth will need to do their share, especially the wealthiest few.

The recession of 2008 should have taught us not to tolerate banks that are too big to fail. Instead, they were allowed to grow larger. But simply making them smaller won't fix the problem. Ben Bernanke makes a good point that size can have benefits in providing services that smaller organizations can't. We have to look beyond size at how companies are organized and at their services. The goal should be to promote competition and to ensure that financial institutions can cover the risks they take. Those who yammer for an unregulated market must accept that in such markets failure is a real possibility and there are no government bail-outs. It's true that such bail-outs minimized the severity of the 2008 recession, but companies must not expect future bail-outs from their greedy foolishness.

It's not just financial organizations that have become unwieldy, however. The technology sector is ripe for trust busting interventions. Wheeler recommends monitoring social media through "public interest algorithms." These would allow them to learn, "who purchased ads or created a post—and combining that with information about reach, engagement, and demographics—would allow a public interest algorithm to assemble a picture of what is being spread and to which communities."

This is a good idea but it doesn't go far enough. Solutions to monopolies like Facebook are not likely to be simple, but they are urgently needed. It may also be necessary to break the hold of operating systems such as Windows by putting their core code either in the public domain or by nationalizing it. And as mentioned earlier, patents are far too easily granted and far too strictly enforced. Fresh ideas and new competitors must

We Can Fix It

be encouraged and, to do this, unfair business barriers must be curtailed.

We also need to prepare for a future in which robotics and artificial intelligence will play a great part. We may need to implement a universal income, but at the very least we will need to retrain our workforce. Imagine a country that encourages creative competition as well as cooperation by subsidizing education for certificates or degrees and start-up funding for groups creating socially-beneficial enterprises. That's not what we have currently, but it's what we desperately need.

We need to go in a different direction than the one where the 2017 tax act will take us. Fixing that tax law could take time. When Ronald Reagan signed his tax reform bill in 1986, it had been under development for two years. The 2017, in contrast, was assembled in a slap-dash manner in a few months. It was mostly a shopping list for the superwealthy. Repairing it will require thought.

There are three types of taxes: progressive, regressive, and proportional or flat. The Social Security tax could be considered a proportional tax, however some consider it to be regressive because income is no longer taxed above $128,400. Those of high income are spared this tax. I hope that the 2017 tax act is repealed, however there's another way to fund programs that create opportunities through education and business creation. If we eliminated the income cap on its taxation, Social Security might not only be solvent, but paying for other programs as well.

Currently we live in a country where many face growing uncertainly about their future job prospects, health care costs, and retirement survivability. In their speeches, Abraham Lincoln and Theodore Roosevelt state that those unwilling to work shouldn't be handed a living. But they also favor a level playing field on which those who are willing to strive can achieve prosperity.

Getting Even

The future will not be easy. Seven billion earthly residents put a strain on our environment and what happens afar will also affect those of us at home. While no one deserves a free lunch, no one deserves to have hurdles placed in front of them either. We need to remove such basic hurdles as access to healthcare and job training. We need to build a country in which the American Dream is achievable once more.

Book and Journal Sources

Anderson, Kurt. "How America Lost Its Mind." *The Atlantic,* September 2017 Vol. 320—No. 2

Drum, Kevin. "You Will Lose Your Job to a Robot." *Mother Jones,* November + December, 2017

Eagleman, David M. "Incognito : The Secret Lives of the Brain." Pantheon, 2011

Fisher, Mattew, et al. "The Tribalism of Truth." *Scientific American*, February 2018

Fitzgerald, Jay. "Robots and Jobs in the U.S. Labor Market." *The NBER Digest,* May 2017

Frase, Peter. *Four Futures : Visions of the World After Capitalism.* (Jacobin) Penguin Random House Publisher Services, 2016.

Fraser, Steve. *The Age of Acquiescence : The Life and Death of American Resistance to Organized Wealth and Power.* Little, Brown and Company, 2015

Hacker, Jacob S. and Pierson, Paul. *Winner-Take-All Politics : How Washington Made the Rich Richer And Turned Its Back on the Middle Class.* Simon & Schuster, 2010

Hedges, Chris. *Unspeakable : Chris Hedges on the Most Forbidden Topics in America with David Talbot.* Hot Books, 2016

We Can Fix It

Krugman, Paul R. *The Conscience of a Liberal.* W.W. Norton & Co., 2007

Levitan, Dave. *Not a scientist : how politicians mistake, misrepresent, and utterly mangle science.* W.W. Norton & Company, 2017

Lindsey, Brink and Teles, Steven. *The Captured Economy : How the Powerful Enrich Themselves, Slow Down Growth, and Increase Inequality.* Oxford University Press, 2017

Mayer, Jane. *Dark Money: The Hidden History of the Billionaires Behind the Rise of the Radical Right.* Doubleday, 2016

Quattrociocchi, Walter. "Inside The Echo Chamber." *Scientific American,* vol. 316, issue 4, 03/2017

Reich, Robert B. *Saving Capitalism : For the many, not the few.* Alfred A. Knopf, 2015

Scheidel, Walter. *The Great Leveler : Violence and the History of Inequality from the Stone Age to the Twenty-first Century.* Princeton University Press, 2017.

Shapiro, Thomas M. *Toxic inequality : how America's wealth gap destroys mobility, deepens the racial divide, & threatens our future.* Basic Books, 2017

Sifry, Micah L. "Antitrust Facebook." *Nation.* 10/30/2017, Vol. 305, Issue 11

Sitaraman, Ganesh. *The crisis of the middle class constitution : why economic inequality threatens our Republic.* Alfred A. Knopf, 2017

Book and Journal Sources

Snyder, Timothy. *On Tyranny : Twenty Lessons from the Twentieth Century.* Tim Duggan Books, 2017

Vedantam, Shankar. *The Hidden Brain : How our Unconscious Minds Elect Presidents, Control Markets, and Save our Lives.* Spiegel & Grau, 2010

Williams, Joan C. *White Working Class : Overcoming Class Cluelessness in America.* Harvard Business Review Press, 2017

Wright, Robert. Why Buddhism is true. Simon & Schuster, 2017

Web Sources

In the order used or referenced

On the Lifeboat
Can ExxonMobil be Found Liable for Misleading the Public on Climate Change?" *Bloomberg.com*, September 7, 2016, http://www.bloomberg.com/news/articles/2016-09-07/will-exxonmobil-have-to-pay-for-misleading-the-public-on-climate-change

Barrett, Paul and Matthew Philips. ""Scientific Consensus: Earth's Climate is Warming." *nasa.gov*, http://climate.nasa.gov/scientific-consensus/

Alston, Philip. "Statement on Visit to the USA, by Professor Philip Alston, United Nations Special Rapporteur on extreme poverty and human rights." *ohchr.org*, December 15, 2017, http://www.ohchr.org/EN/NewsEvents/Pages/DisplayNews.aspx?NewsID=22533&LangID=E

Rhodes, Joshua. "Solar Tariff Is a Direct Hit to Fastest-Growing Job in U.S." *forbes.com*, January 23, 2018, http://www.forbes.com/sites/joshuarhodes/2018/01/23/solar-tariff-a-direct-hit-to-fastest-growing-job-market-in-us/

Lee, Michelle Hee Ye. "Koch network to spend about another $20 million promoting GOP tax law." *washingtonpost.com*, January 27, 2018, http://www.washingtonpost.com/news/powerpost/wp/2018/01/27/koch-network-to-spend-up-to-20-

million-promoting-gop-tax-law/

Kurtzleben, Danielle. "Charts: See How Much of GOP Tax Cuts Will Go to the Middle Class." *npr.org*, December 19, 2017, http://www.npr.org/2017/12/19/571754894/charts-see-how-much-of-gop-tax-cuts-will-go-to-the-middle-class

A Broken Dream
"OECD Income Distribution Database (IDD): Gini, poverty, income, Methods and Concepts." oecd.org, http://www.oecd.org/social/income-distribution-database.htm

Jefferson, Thomas. "Letter to Madison." *teachingamericanhistory.org,* http://teachingamericanhistory.org/library/document/jefferson-to-madison/

Lincoln, Abraham. "Lincoln's Milwaukee Speech." *nal.usda.gov* (USDA National Agricultural Library), http://www.nal.usda.gov/lincolns-milwaukee-speech

A Bit of History
Roosevelt, Theodore. "From the Archives: President Teddy Roosevelt's New Nationalism Speech" obamawhitehouse.archives.gov, http://obamawhitehouse.archives.gov/blog/2011/12/06/archives-president-teddy-roosevelts-new-nationalism-speech

Smith, Richard Norton and Walch, Timothy. "The Ordeal of Herbert Hoover." *archives.gov* (Prologue Magazine), 2004, http://www.archives.gov/publications/prologue/2004/

summer/hoover-1.html

Roosevelt, Franklin D. "Campaign Address on Progressive Government at the Commonwealth Club in San Francisco." *Presidency.ucsb.edu*, http://www.presidency.ucsb.edu/ws/?pid=88391

A Middle Bulges Before Belts Tighten
National Labor Relations Board. "Interfering with employee rights (Section 7 & 8(a)(1))." *Nlrb.gov*, http://www.nlrb.gov/rights-we-protect/whats-law/employers/interfering-employee-rights-section-7-8a1

Murrow, Edward R. "Murrow on McCarthy, no fear, 1954." *youtube.com*, http://www.youtube.com/watch?v=vEvEmkMNYHY

Eisenhower, Dwight. "To Edgar Newton Eisenhower." *web.archive.org*, http://web.archive.org/web/20051124190902/http://www.eisenhowermemorial.org/presidential-papers/first-term/documents/1147.cfm

Felzenberg, Alvin "The Inside Story of William F. Buckley Jr.'s Crusade against the John Birch Society." *nationalreview.com*, June, 20 2017, http://www.nationalreview.com/article/448774/william-f-buckley-john-birch-society-history-conflict-robert-welch

Chad Mitchell Trio, "The John Birch Society" *youtube.com,* http://www.youtube.com/watch?v=6VRWWxMDmCQ

Dickinson, Tom. "Inside the Koch Brothers' Toxic Empire." *rollingstone.com*, September, 2014, http://www.rollingstone.com/politics/news/inside-the-koch-brothers-toxic-empire-20140924

O'Harrow, Robert Jr. "A two-decade crusade by conservative charities fueled Trump's exit from Paris climate accord." *washingtonpost.com*, September 5, 2017, http://www.washingtonpost.com/investigations/a-two-decade-crusade-by-conservative-charities-fueled-trumps-exit-from-paris-climate-accord/2017/09/05/fcb8d9fe-6726-11e7-9928-22d00a47778f_story.html

Oxfam International. "Just eight men own same wealth as half the world." *oxfam.org*, January, 1917, http://www.oxfam.org/en/pressroom/pressreleases/2017-01-16/just-8-men-own-same-wealth-half-world

Bruenig, Matt. "Wealth Inequality Is Higher Than Ever." *jacobinmag.com,* October, 2017, http://www.jacobinmag.com/2017/10/wealth-inequality-united-states-federal-reserve

"United States Net Worth Brackets, Percentiles, and Top One Percent in 2017." *dqydj.com,* http://dqydj.com/net-worth-brackets-wealth-brackets-one-percent/

Fear the Robots
Deaderick, Jen. "Robots and Jobs in the U.S. Labor Market." nber.org, May, 2017, http://www.nber.org/digest/may17/may17.pdf

"Figures at a glance." *unhcr.org* The UN Refugee Agency, http://www.unhcr.org/en-us/figures-at-a-glance.html

Web Sources

The Silenced Majority
Totenberg, Nina "When Did Companies Become People? Excavating The Legal Evolution." npr.org, July 24, 2014,
http://www.npr.org/2014/07/28/335288388/when-did-companies-become-people-excavating-the-legal-evolution

McElroy, Lisa. "Citizens United v. FEC in plain English." *scotusblog.com*, January 22, 2010,
http://www.scotusblog.com/2010/01/citizens-united-v-fec-in-plain-english/

Weintraub, Ellen L. "Taking On Citizens United." *nytimes.com*, March 3, 2016,
http://www.nytimes.com/2016/03/30/opinion/taking-n-citizens-united.html

Krueger, Alan B. "Economic Scene; The many faces of Adam Smith: Rediscovering 'The Wealth of Nations.'" *nytimes.com,* August 16, 2001,
http://www.nytimes.com/2001/08/16/business/economic-scene-the-many-faces-of-adam-smith-rediscovering-the-wealth-of-nations.html

Follow the Money
Risen, James. "Investigation Into Missing Iraqi Cash Ended in Lebanon Bunker." *nytimes.com* October 12, 2014,
http://www.nytimes.com/2014/10/12/world/investigation-into-missing-iraqi-cash-ended-in-lebanon-bunker.html

Bush, George W. "Selected Speeches of George W. Bush 2001—2008." *georgewbush-whitehouse.archives.gov*, http://georgewbush-whitehouse.archives.gov/infocus/bushrecord/documents/Selected_Speeches_George_W_Bush.pdf

Bernanke, Ben S. "Ending 'too big to fail': What's the right approach." *brookings.edu,* May 13, 2016, http://www.brookings.edu/blog/ben-bernanke/2016/05/13/ending-too-big-to-fail-whats-the-right-approach/

Merle, Renae. "House passes sweeping legislation to roll back banking rules." *washingtonpost.com,* June 9, 2017, http://www.washingtonpost.com/news/wonk/wp/2017/06/08/house-to-vote-on-sweeping-rollback-of-banking-rules/

Cassidy, John. "The Final G.O.P. Tax Bill Is a Recipe for Even More Inequality." *newyorker.com,* December 14, 2017, http://www.newyorker.com/news/our-columnists/the-final-gop-tax-bill-is-a-recipe-for-even-more-inequality

Cooperation or Chaos?
Scheidel, Walter. "Column: The only conquerors of inequality are the Four Horsemen of the Apocalypse." *pbs.org,* June 16,2017, http://www.pbs.org/newshour/economy/column-conquerors-inequality-four-horsemen-apocalypse

Know Your Enemy
Martin, Michel (interviewing Wu, Frank). "30 Years Later, Vincent Chin Seen As Turning Point." *npr.org,* July 2, 2012, http://www.npr.org/2012/07/02/156121146/30-years-later-vincent-chin-seen-as-turning-point

Web Sources

Irwin, Neil. "We're Getting Awfully Close to Full Employment." *nytimes.com*, May 5, 2017, http://www.nytimes.com/2017/05/05/upshot/were-getting-awfully-close-to-full-employment.html

Krogstad, Jens Manuel, Passel, Jeffrey S. and Cohn, D'Vera. "5 facts about illegal immigration in the U.S." *pewresearch.org*, April 27, 2017, http://www.pewresearch.org/fact-tank/2017/04/27/5-facts-about-illegal-immigration-in-the-u-s/

Neel, Joe. "Poll: Most Americans Think Their Own Group Faces Discrimination." npr.org, October 24, 2017, http://www.npr.org/sections/health-shots/2017/10/24/559116373/poll-most-americans-think-their-own-group-faces-discrimination

Weapons of Mass Deception
Arnold, Carrie. "Diss Information: Is There a Way to Stop Popular Falsehoods from Morphing into "Facts"?" *scientificamerican.com*, October 2012, http://www.scientificamerican.com/article/how-to-stop-misinformation-from-becoming-popular-belief/

Martucci, Katherine. "Anxious? Activate Your Anterior Cingulate Cortex With a Little Meditation." wakehealth.edu, 2013, http://www.wakehealth.edu/News-Releases/2013/Anxious_Activate_Your_Anterior_Cingulate_Cortex_With_a_Little_Meditation.htm

Mitchell, Amy, et al. "How Americans Encounter, Recall and Act Upon Digital News" journalism.org, February 9 2017, http://www.journalism.org/2017/02/09/how-americans-encounter-recall-and-act-upon-digital-news/

Wheeler, Tom. "Did technology kill the truth?" brookings.edu, November 14, 2017, http://www.brookings.edu/research/did-technology-kill-the-truth/

Wexler, Celia Viggo. "The Fallout From the Telecommunications Act of 1996: Unintended Consequences and Lessons Learned." *commoncause.org,* May 9, 2005, http://www.commoncause.org/research-reports/National_050905_Fallout_From_The_Telecommunications_Act_2.pdf

Getting Even
Budiansky, Stephen. "Adam Smith, Thomas Jefferson, and other fellow travelers." *Budiansky.blogspot.com,* October 14, 2010, http://budiansky.blogspot.com/2010/10/adam-smith-thomas-jefferson-and-other.html

Henry-Nickie, Makada. "Leveraging the disruptive power of artificial intelligence for fairer opportunities." brookings.edu, November 16, 2017, http://www.brookings.edu/blog/techtank/2017/11/16/leveraging-the-disruptive-power-of-artificial-intelligence-for-fairer-opportunities/

www.ingramcontent.com/pod-product-compliance
Lightning Source LLC
Chambersburg PA
CBHW020427220526
45464CB00002B/599